MINISTERING TO YOUTH

MINISTERING TO YOUTH

A Guide For Parents, Teachers and Youth Workers

by Michael G. Wensing

Library of Congress Cataloging in Publication Data

Wensing, Michael G.
  Ministering to youth.

  Includes bibliographical references.
  1. Church work with youth—Catholic Church.
  2. Catholic Church—Education. 1. Title.
  BX2347.8.Y7W44   1982   259'.23   82-11382
  ISBN 0-8189-0444-5

Nihil Obstat:
James Joyce
Censor Librorum

Imprimatur:
†Paul V. Dudley
Bishop of Sioux Falls
April 14, 1982

Designed, printed and bound in the United States of
America by the Fathers and Brothers of the
Society of St. Paul, 2187 Victory Boulevard,
Staten Island, New York 10314, as part of their
communications apostolate.

2 3 4 5 6 7 8 9 (Current Printing: first digit).

The intent of this book is to aid parents, youth workers, priests, sisters, brothers and anyone else involved in any form of youth work to grow in their own joy about the work they are doing and to become re-converted to this all important ministry. Thus the book combines some personal experiences, some academic understandings about youth themselves as well as ministry to them, and some spiritual guidance. It is a garden variety of wisdom gained by one youth director willingly shared so that others may know the graciousness of the God we all share in common.

TABLE OF CONTENTS

INTRODUCTION

COME, O HOLY SPIRIT, COME.
COME AS THE WIND AND CLEANSE;
COME AS THE FIRE AND BURN;
CONVERT AND CONSECRATE OUR LIVES
TO OUR GREAT GOOD AND YOUR GREAT GLORY;
THROUGH JESUS CHRIST OUR LORD. AMEN*

Enthusiastic, sad, full of zip, jubilant, joyful, excited, impassioned—are all qualities descriptive of youth. Amazingly, these are also qualities that can be attributed to the Holy Spirit. As a Christian leader I could never hope to understand the culture of the youth, or stand up before them to speak, or mingle with them, unless I first approached the Holy Spirit. It is the Spirit of God which gives us understanding to work with the youth of any age.

We perceive the larger images of the Trinity at work all around us as revealed by the Holy Spirit. The image of the Father is seen most evident in those who stand before us as heroes, in those who are leaders, in those who initiate, and in those who create. The image of Jesus is seen most evident in those who witness strongly the power of God in their lives, in those who show compassion for the poorer among us. But the

---

* from the *Notre Dame Prayerbook for Students,* p. 39, Ave Maria Press, Notre Dame, Indiana, 1975.

image of the Spirit is seen naturally in the idealism of youth, in their passion to know and have life to the fullest. Of course, we believe everyone is, under the grace of God, a temple of the Holy Spirit. Yet, the unique qualities of the Holy Spirit show forth in the human vessels of the youth like no other age group.

This must be the irresistible force that makes so many older adults want to associate with the young people of their lives. But there is likewise the force that threatens to become corrupt, wild, and uncontrolled, and thereby frightens many of the same older adults into keeping themselves apart from the younger generation. We need to pray to the Holy Spirit for guidance, pray to the Holy Spirit for wisdom and understanding, and pray to the Holy Spirit for real strength before the wild testings and challenging questions of the young. Real understanding, real strength of conviction are deeply wanted by the young, though sorely tested for their authenticity.

There is no greater quality of work with youth than a clarity of vision. Personality may awe them for a short while, vision guides them. Great talent may draw them, vision keeps them. Reputation they will want to check out, vision they will want to understand. Nothing can be shared quite like a vision. Personality and talent and reputation are very special gifts indeed, but are personally possessed. Vision can be captured and be had equally by all. A clarity of vision of Jesus and a clarity of vision of the Church is qualification number one for any leader or parent or teacher to work successfully with youth. And such a vision is truly the workings of the Holy Spirit within a Christian leader's life. Contemplate the Holy Spirit who brings us the Word of God. Contemplate the Holy Spirit who moves persons to search out Jesus and His Church, who moves persons who want to understand that special Person and His bride, the Church, who moves such persons to accept that which they have found.

God is the source of all life. The Father creates life, the Son redeems life, and the Holy Spirit gives life a capital L —Life in its fullest. And there is no other age group quite so excited about the fullness of life as youth. How exciting it can be to be a part of that passion for life lived to its fullest. How needed are those adults who can share a vision of life that is full of God, and that life cannot be full except with God square in the middle of it. It was St. Ireneaus who said that the Glory of God is man fully alive. And life is for the glory of God. The glory of God flows out of those who have truly made themselves, no, allowed themselves, to be true temples of the Holy Spirit.

I pray the Holy Spirit to guide my sharing on His work come alive in youth.

MINISTERING TO YOUTH

A Guide For Parents, Teachers and Youth Workers

Chapter One

FIRED UP

Dear God,

I got left back. Thanks a lot.

Raymond

Dear God,

Are you real? Some people don't believe it.
If you are, you better do something quick.

Harriet Ann

(from *Children's Letters to God*, published
by Pocket Books, NY)

October 18, 12:45 AM

Dear Father Mike,

Hello! I'm sorry this letter is on notebook paper, but this promises to be an extremely long letter and my little 4″ × 6″ paper just wouldn't be able to take it. The friction from my pen would probably make it burn or something.

I am currently lying on my cot, listening to Billy Joel tell me why I'm *not* going to die young and I have a lovely glass of chocolate milk by my side. I always eat something when I'm depressed, which doesn't really make much sense at all, because I'll really be depressed when I weigh 300 lbs. Anyway, what I'm trying to say is that I'm very comfortable and I suggest you get into the same state of laid back. Pull up a pew and stretch out, or something. As I said before, this promises to be a very long letter.

First of all, Fr. V. sends his greetings. I tackled him in the hall for your address. There are a few things you just gotta learn about people like me. I guess the best place to start is the way I got this address from Father V. Do you remember the scene in the movie *The Godfather* where the movie director wakes up and finds a horse's head between the sheets? Well, I threatened to do the same with Fr. V.'s transmission.

Seriously, Father, I have always been very honest in my emotions; I just don't like hiding something that is such a part of me. It's one of the reasons Fr. V. can't stand me; he doesn't like what he calls my "moodiness." Too bad, huh?

If I am going to remain honest in my emotions, I've got to tell you about what seeing you at the local Youth Rally did to me. It scared me. You see, Father, when you were at our junior class retreat last year and I gave you all that trouble, it was the beginning of a very bad time for me. It was all my fault, of course, but that's beside the point. The whole situation was the straw that broke the horse's back for Mr. R., the principal, and Father V. They called my parents into school and Fr. V. told my folks that I was "gross, obscene and unladylike." This publicity shamed my parents, although they didn't show it at the time, hence some of my hair was cut off. It's the old custom of public shame for public shame.

While Fr. V. was merrily telling my folks what a rotten person I am, Mr. R. was telling them that he just couldn't "take any more." I've been in trouble before, you see, because I come under the heading of "one of the dregs of society." Mr. R. said that he would decide whether to start expulsion proceedings or not.

So while he's deciding, I'm sitting at home with a shorn head and a brand-new ulcer. I decided enough was enough and planned out the best way to kill myself. You see, it was three days I was waiting to hear Mr. R.'s decision. I had it all planned out. I make a lot of jokes about my suicide attempt now (I tried to kill myself once by walking in front of a parked car, etc.). At the time I was very serious. Anyway, Mr. R. called Ma and told her he had decided *not* to expel me.

I was relieved until about three weeks later when I was talking to another faculty member. I found out they never intended to expel me. They just set up the whole thing to "teach me a lesson" and "make me sweat a little." Believe me Father, it was not myself I wanted to kill by then.

So here it is, five months or so later and I see you at this rally. I tensed up and was in considerable pain. During all that time I spent on the bleachers, I just waited for you to see me and denounce me to the populace. I expected it, I waited for it and it didn't come.

So, after Mass, I decided to throw my favorite motto— "Cowardice is the better part of valor" out of the window. I decided to talk to you and at least tell you that I enjoyed the rally and the Mass. I was certain you wouldn't remember me.

You remembered me; you shouldn't have but you did. You not only remembered me, but you seemed genuinely happy to see me. You hugged me. Freaky! No one reacts to me that way . . . my teachers who say they like me, always greet me with apprehension. I don't blame them; I'm a spooky sort of person. But when you greeted me and talked to me as you did, it gave me a sense of incredible happiness.

Listen to me, Father, I may be only seventeen, but in that time I have seen much. I was once told by an exasperated nun, who was trying desperately to get me to "confide" in her, that I am "seventeen going on forty." So take it from a forty-year-old, don't associate with sinners. We're bad news.

I am told that I have changed from what I was. Perhaps, perhaps not. Ha, I know that I have given up my dream of changing the Catholic Church all by myself. You'll notice it didn't work; you're not speaking Hebrew when you say Mass. That was my plan, you see.

If I have read your character correctly, you will be concerned about me. Don't waste the time. I not only can take care of myself, I do take care of myself. I get hurt, but I'm alive; the hurts have made me strong.

Peace and love
Maria
Rebel without a cause

PS Keep your head down

In a way this book is about Maria and about many more. These are the youth who are searching in this modern world for so much and receiving so little from that modern world, so little from "out there." And the meaning they are looking for, as we all are, is the meaning of Christ. That meaning, let me be bold to say, is still found "within the Church." It is found through a community of believers—through committed others. It is still our faith that the meaning of Christ is to be found also "within" one's self by way of example, love, and witnessing of a community of believers.

I received this letter from Maria some eight months after I first met her. I had wanted to forget the former occasion as soon as possible. It was a high school retreat day that I had been asked to conduct. There was a group of some one hundred juniors in high school all crowded into one room loaned to us by a nearby college. Some minutes after the day officially began, in the middle of some light hearted introductory remarks, a young lady came sauntering in, chewing gum, and wearing a pre-meditated bored look. On her way back to the last row of chairs in the room she made some remark like "oh yuk." There were enough chuckles from the others to encourage her to go on during the day with many other attention getting devices appropriately timed to throw off some of the major points I was making in the retreat. I was undone by the events taking place, and since this was not my usual high school classroom where such happenings were taken care of immediately, I knew this was a day to weather and make the most of, in any event.

I was taken back in memory many years to the time in the later 1960's when I had just begun my college seminary program. As it was appropriate for each student to volunteer to do some charitable work once a week outside of the seminary, I volunteered to help teach a CCD class at a parish in a nearby rural town. I was just a sophomore in college and was given a class of 20 sophomores and juniors barely three years younger than myself. What a mistake that was for everyone. My most easily retrieved memory of the experience was the incident of the goldfish spearing contest. Several ringleaders planned a contest to coincide with the first handing out of pencils (freshly sharpened) for a quiz. The year ended with less than 10 of the original 20 present due to choice on their part and disciplinary reaction on my part. Oh yes, a dozen goldfish in an aquarium which someone had donated to the parish, stored in my room, was reduced to six. In my book CCD was not the initials for Confraternity of Christian Doctrine but was better re-abbreviated Christian Combat Duty.

This incident of a year of teaching and several related incidences thoroughly convinced me that youth work was a calling I was to avoid at all costs. I might have lost my early desires for the priesthood as well, if I did not have before me exemplary priests doing many things in their ministry that did not include youth. That would be the way I would have to be a priest, my disillusionment reasoned.

Others have similar stories to tell of their experiences and they make for good war stories at a gathering of ex-teachers and volunteers. Thus I did effectively avoid formal contact with youth of younger than college age for five years as I busily worked to complete my theology degree.

Inevitably, as it seems now, I was drawn into youth work through the back door. I had been feverishly buried in the books for two years in theology when something inside ached for outside involvement with lots of life, lots of faith, lots of mixed people, (especially women and men as I was in an environment totally comprised only of men). A classmate invited me to go downtown with him to the Catholic Youth Center to a prayer meeting on Tuesday evening. "This is different than you may expect" he stated. "It isn't just a small youth prayer group." I was willing as I hadn't found my outside involvement yet even after visiting hospital programs and parish settings.

Weird! That is all I could seem to think to describe what I saw and heard. The gathering at the prayer group was five hundred plus strong and 75% were young people between the ages of 17 and 25. They were singing the most exciting music, laughing freely and shouting "Praise the Lord." It was the breaking out in tongues that completely threw me. This was so foreign to my Germanic background and stoic parish experience under the pastorship of a Polish priest that I wanted to run. It was even foreign to my seminary experiences. Yet as young men or young women will say about persons they are falling in love with "That person bothers me," I felt the irresistible attraction to have more of this despite its great "bothersomeness."

After six months of "standing off" as objective person, I was taken into a retreat experience with the community that became my official entry into participation in the community as responsible member. I was hooked. Before long I was staffing weekend retreats for youth, doing counseling and having a lot of fun at coffeehouse nights and dances. There was a new sense of freedom being a part of this community. But most fortunate of all, two long-standing crises of my vocation were being healed—celibacy and my feelings about youth work.

The Gospel of St. John relates an incident about the importance of someone or something being the instrument, the go-between, of our ideals and affections. In John 1:35 Jesus comes on the scene and seemingly there is no great excitement. John the Baptist points out to his disciples that this was the one everybody was waiting for. It was then that two disciples of his became curious and checked Jesus out. "Come and see" was Jesus' invitation to their curiosity. And we know the rest of the story. They were hooked.

My bishop assigned me after a year of parish work as a priest to teach in a local private high school. I was as angry as could be. It was my fear, but I did not know it then, and so in my anger I sought out the bishop and asked him why he didn't consult me on how I felt about such a thing. Yet he was a John the Baptist for me. He pointed out the path I was to take and once I investigated it I was hooked. Within a year a new bishop decided to form a youth office for the first time in the diocese to help guide all the new developments of TEC, SEARCH, etc. that were rapidly growing in our midst. This unwilling and fearful priest got his letter of assignment to the directorship of the office. God has His plans and sometimes uses all kinds of back doors to bring us to the place he wants us to be. What a blessed ministry it is to bring the good news of God's kingdom to the searching, listening ears of youth. It is *1 John* come alive: "What we have seen and heard we proclaim in turn to you so that you may share life with us."

Back to Maria. This was more a lesson for me than anything. There is the old cliché that you can love a person into change quicker than you can drive them into change. As an outside retreat master I had the perfect chance to act on this truism. When I heard the words "Oh yuk" the immediate reaction was to recoil and avoid confrontation with this "nut." Otherwise my temper would be engaged and the mood of the retreat would be totally different, raising impossible obstacles to openness to anything I might have to say that day. Yet I knew there was another approach that deserved my greatest effort. It is no secret. Good youth workers, effective with youth, have known this for a long time. The challenge in this case is to become completely solicitous of such a person. Take every opportunity at breaks, with eye contact, compliments, etc. to build up the person who has confronted you or challenged you. One feels a little awkward in the beginning for the natural feelings of anger and the urge to recoil are prevalent. However, you put those feelings on the back burner for the time being and resolve to discuss that with the person at some later date. You just love in every word and act you are capable of at the moment. I have seen this work wonders in the past and am still seeing it work miracles today. It definitely means you go against the grain of normal human interaction for awhile. Yet that is precisely why this encouragement works so well. It breaks the script that others are used to acting out. They know what the normal reaction is to their antics and comments. They expect these reactions and when something different comes instead they are faced with new choices, thoughts, and even behaviors.

The day did not end all that much better in this situation with Maria. However, later at the rally as Maria's letter mentioned, I was greeting the people afterwards when Maria came through the crowd. I reached around a couple of people and caught hold of an arm and pulled her over for a hug and a few words in the midst of the crowd pushing past. It made all the difference for the both of us. The feelings of anger and discouragement I had left on the back burner had dissolved somewhere along the line and never had to be discussed. Maria in many more later letters announced great steps of growth with teachers, parents, and grades. A new cycle of growth had been unleashed. She saw her talents in writing and has since gone into journalism and adds creative touches to retreat programs and liturgies and study groups that she is a part of in some regular fashion.

I used to get so depressed over my lack of talents. Most people believe you need rich and impressive talents to do effective youth work. My friend Gary can play a guitar with great ability. He can strap on a mouth organ like Bob Dylan and sing, and play, and harmonize like no one else I know. I admire Gary. But I am even more jealous of him than admiring on many days because I think I should have a talent such as singing or a musical ability, for nothing has such a good effect on young people as impressive music. Gary can put on a good modern record and play and sing in harmony with it in unison with the band or singer on the recording. What talent! And yet I have not been able to figure out why he is not interested in youth work. Then there is Phil. He has a great clown skit going. He can alter his approach from clowning to mime and physically is as limber as spiderman. Fortunately, he likes youth work and is one of God's great instruments in this area. But why couldn't I be as creative as Phil and have such a great drawing card as he has in his clowning. And there is Ann. Can she ever tell stories that has everyone on the edge of their seats or else rolling on the floor with laughter. What a delight to listen to her speak. It has been my good fortune to have Ann work on team with me at retreat evenings and weekends. I hope she sees what a great gift God gave her and uses it in powerful ways for the Lord. But then I still feel the twinge of envy for some outstanding talent as that.

This is common reasoning among so many adults concerning youth work. Either there is a jealousy for great talent or there is tremendous inferiority over a self-perceived lack of such. Thus you have the statements: "I could never do that kind of work," "I don't want to do it," or "I refuse to do it," or "I am scared to touch it." This is normal feeling behind such statements or reasonings. Now feelings are neither right nor wrong, they just are. Once we recognize them, then we can look closer at their cause or basis and do something about it. It is the decision and action flowing from them that can be right action or wrong action. Thus, youth work or youth concern follows a basic decision just to do something or just to be concerned and open to opportunities. The same goes for relating to and working with any segment of humanity: children, the elderly, parents, professionals, or our own age group. We begin by placing our hearts and minds in the right direction and take every opportunity for education, growth, and relating.

My conversion to youth work was not a discovery of talents that I wished I had (though in the process I did discover some storytelling ability, some music ability, some insight ability) but a discovery of the love Christ placed in my heart that needed to be expressed, trusted, and acted upon. We are not to worry about our weakness for God surprises us in this as He did St.

Paul who said "In my weakness I am made strong."

A good weakness humored is an act of love for it tells others what it means to say "I'm loveable despite my weakness." Everyone can appreciate a person who laughs at himself. We identify with that person for we all have characteristics about ourselves we can laugh over or wish we could. I have a friend who gets more laughs over his baldness. He will begin a sharing or speech by telling the audience he would like to give a little reflection off the top of his head. Or he will put on an Afro wig and speak as if nothing has changed about his appearance. Then there is another person who has gone from a self-consciousness about her shortness to making it a laughing matter. She will make comments like "Let me tell you a tall story." There really is not weakness in either of these examples but often we perceive them to be just that when we look at ourselves.

We need to realize that what truly needs to be laughed at is the pre-conceived ideal we have of what an American male or an American woman is to look like, act like, dress like, etc. Humor breaks those stereotype expectations we hold toward ourselves and lifts up the dignity of the true person beneath the physical appearance. That is true if the person can laugh at himself or herself and initiates the sharing with such wit. It is not anything less than cruel if someone laughs at another person with put-down statements. That is obvious enough.

The basic value one must hold to begin youth work is not the possession of many talents but the self perception that "I am loveable and capable." There are a lot of little pamphlets floating around with a front picture of a cartoon person carrying a sign with the word IALAC written on the banner. Succinctly the pamphlet portrays how we get up in the morning and begin putting ourselves and the day down until we fulfill those very expectations of awfulness about ourselves and the day. It is negative thinking, or, as people involved in Alcoholics Anonymous say "stinking thinking." We are to rise in the morning and put on our imaginary IALAC sign or button and begin the day with positive thoughts about all the possibilities of giving and loving before us as well as filling our minds and hearts with the expectation of good that will come our way in that day. IALAC (I am loveable and capable) is to become YALAC (You are loveable and capable) when we encounter others. Youth work and/or any effective ministry requires us to move from the core self attitude of IALAC to YALAC. There is a dictum that you cannot give what you do not first possess. We have already discussed that we have God's love within. The next possession is self-love. Then other-love is possible.

With the possession of IALAC we can move to YALAC which is the center of ministry to youth. In myriad ways the youth minister shows the young person how they are very loveable and filled with capability. In this way the young person can begin to wear their IALAC button and move to YALAC with their peers, and even their parents and teachers. Thus the chain of christian love is started and continues. And St. Paul tells of Charity that it is the greatest reality of Christianity even when it stands in comparison to the greatness of Faith and Hope.

This is where the purveyors of positive thinking with their expensive programs and Christianity share such common ground. A believer can and should make great use of this art of positive thinking not to conquer the world and be a financial success but in order to give, in order to love. The reality of IALAC was basic to my life and work and acceptance of youth ministry. And it was basic to my conversion to full love of what I do and am. How the Lord has blessed this guy! The truest joy comes when you see YALAC truly work. The other person begins to share faith they did not know they had, they listen and visit with their parents as another equal adult. They begin to volunteer for things within the Church and outside the Church. Their school work improves as does their relationship with the teachers. Things make sense to them in their real world. Not everything is senseless any longer outside of the world of their immediate friends.

The great mystics of my faith came to a conclusion about all this in their prayer. Their conclusion and discovery was that creation is gracious, reality is gracious. That is, it is a gift of God for us to enjoy. St. Theresa said it well when she stated that everything is grace. Thus the source of IALAC and YALAC is the graciousness of God. You are a grace and so is everyone you come into contact with, as is every situation through which you come into contact with those others. Every work, every person, is filled with loveableness and capacity for greatness. Praise God! God can use me. God can use you.

Chapter Two

A CLARITY OF VISION

A new springtime is among us. Jesus said: "Remember the fig tree and all the other trees. When you see the leaves beginning to appear you know that summer is near" (Lk 21:30). The springtime of a new youth population in and out of our Churches is present everywhere. The building signs are there for anyone immersed this past decade in youth work in any form. What are the leaf signs of this springtime? Let us take a look.

During the 60's and 70's I can easily remember the dualism that existed between any authority situation and young people in any given formal setting of school, church, retreat, etc. It was as if as soon as the adult authority stood in the room or began to speak you could see a silent fist knot invisibly in every stomach of youth in the room. At least it seemed that way to many though it was true of only a strong minority within the setting. But the vibrations were felt even from its minor presence. Thus a real challenge existed for the teacher, speaker, parent, minister, religious, or guest visitor who took over in his or her turn rightfully to speak and direct the group present. It was the flavor of the time that heightened the reality of rebellion always present in human beings. It was a tumultuous age in society for one thing. For another thing, as sociologists point out, it was a time when adolescents made up a tremendous bulge in the society. They were the post war baby boom and were just making their numbers felt.

Many left the profession of teaching during these times. Beside hard financial realities this situation aided in the closing of many parochial high schools as well. However, the increase in the number of entrepreneurs in the entertainment world for this age group was significant. Affluence had much to do, along with the leisure time of adolescence, to make restlessness, experimentation and wing testing unavoidable.

The bulge of the war baby boom has left us. That characterizes things differently. We are not dealing with numbers anymore as classroom sizes shrink and schools are re-organizing to handle population shifts and expected slowdowns in student enrollments. Family sizes are smaller. Thus there is once again a higher adult to young people ratio. This allows for more intimate sharing, more individual dialogue between youth and adult.

One of the popular ways of doing youth work in the 60's and 70's was the one on one approach. Youth ministers were withdrawing from formal or traditional programs because of all the difficulties in large group settings and hailing the good effects of one on one. This was true and will always be true. However, the numbers reached are usually small indeed. We have only so much psychic energy to give and can only initiate conversation and new contact so many times in any given day before we turn to the familiar—our regular friends, hobbies, or details and errands, for the rest of the day.

There are plenty of commentaries on the social realities of youth in the years we have just come through. It is more enjoyable and maybe more fruitful to look at what is being observed in the present scene. It is positive and encouraging.

We have among us a more sober group of youth. This is

saying something positive by way of the back door. This could be expected because we have been experiencing some sobering realities in the world and especially the American society. Youth are truly living in a new world. There is a whole new economic situation since 1973 and the oil embargo. Our economy of cheap energy suddenly felt the shock of its own end. It is a fact that we will never return to such cheap energy days when travel, goods, and services were so economical. It will be just plain hard if not impossible to continue the same standard of living we have enjoyed. That is scary to a lot of youth looking hard at their futures. They wish to plan, calculate, and compete early for the best opportunities to keep that life style. The new seriousness sometimes has the drawback of involving young people just into their teens in various jobs, sometimes two or three part-time jobs, when employment is available, to the detriment of higher learning and indepth thought. There is a mad scramble for things and the good times. Thus this seriousness needs to be capitalized upon in such a way that patience is instilled and sacrifice in the present is willingly made for the sake of fuller life later on.

One of the reasons that makes it difficult to urge and encourage sacrifice in the present for the sake of the future is that the future is seen differently now than ever before. There are many youth who honestly do not believe there will be a long future left for the human race, or a future worth living. Their consciousness of the power and destructive capacity of the nuclear age and armaments is so deep and part of their nature that they do not believe we will escape a nuclear showdown within a matter of years. One survey revealed that as high as 80% of high school graduates presently believe that they will not see beyond the year 2000.

During the years of the 1950's many people built fallout shelters in their homes and communities and were consciously storing foodstuffs and water in community fallout centers in preparation for surviving a nuclear war should it come. What with this increased consciousness among our youth one would think there would be a renewed feverish activity about such things once again. Wrong. There was a belief in the 1950's that one could survive a nuclear war if necessary precautions were taken. That belief is shattered among the young today and rightfully so. They take enough science courses and read e-nough literature to know that such preventive measures would be foolish. If one is not hit directly by a bomb, they reason, then the fire and radiation will be lethal within a short time. Or, if by chance the war reigns far off, then the ozone layer would be so destroyed that the sun would effectively kill life on earth. Plant and soil life, as well as water to maintain life, would be spoiled by the effects of radiation. Thus a fatalism exists about the possibility of any kind of survival, or worthy survival, among the present generation of youth.

I have often been in discussions in homes sponsoring youth group activities where this discussion becomes central. The youth take off immediately upon all the ramifications. The adults by and large debate how we need to continue the arms race to protect ourselves. I am amazed at times by the genera-tion gap in this topic where there really are two different understandings. However, adults are becoming more sensitized too.

In any event, this fatalism that can easily surface among youth exerts two different kinds of influences, one, a deep desire to know the spiritual realities of life and the universe, and two, the opposite pressure to enjoy what good times are avail-able now. This pull in two different directions needs to be recognized and then the spiritual pull can be emphasized and magnified so that it becomes the prominent thrust and topic in youth dealings.

The family unit has changed. Besides becoming increas-
ingly smaller numerically many young persons growing up
today do not experience the consistency of having the same
mother and father throughout their childhood and teenage
years. Estimates run near 40% of youth growing up in today's
society having to live through some break-up of the family unit
either temporarily or permanently. That is, a young person will
experience the absence of one parent through death or, more
predominantly, through divorce. Many finish their growing up
years under a single parent and others need to grow comfortable with a new step-parent. Through this process some end
their teen years with a completely different set of parents than
they started with in early childhood.

One of the stunning discoveries of the recent decade
census was the lower than expected population counts in
many areas where there had been an abundant increase of new
homes constructed. This just reflected the pattern of smaller
family units per home and single parenting due to family splits.
It takes many more homes to enclose an equal population than
in years gone by.

This reflection indicates another sobering reality among the
youth population. The desire for family togetherness is strong in
their consciousness. The anxiety over security and future stability in their own lives is a major concern. Thus it is easy to
recognize that you have a more listening audience when you
speak about future concerns and life concerns presently real
which will help or hinder life later on.

All of the above does demonstrate something positive a-
bout work among youth today in that there is a reality of
listening and openness and seriousness which was not there
immediately previous among youth. The faith of the youth
worker is that grace does build on the nature of things. There is
some research that indicates up front a new openness to ritual,

spiritual ideals, prayer, and teachings among the attitudes of youth. Let us take a look at just a couple examples of this research.

The National Opinion Research Center out of Chicago conducted an extensive survey and study of the religious attitudes of the young Catholic Americans and have well publicized their results. Their study covered the age group from sixteen through thirty-five. Those above the age of twenty-one produced different results from those below that age group. There seemed to be more ambivalence among those in the older group concerning the Church and their conception of God. God was seen more in the traditional sense of being judge, supreme authority and rule-giver. This was not universal as many saw God personally and as lover but they were not the majority. There seemed to be a significant difference in attitude toward God among those twenty-one and younger. Their image of God was much softer and God was seen by many with qualities of a mother as well as a loving father. God was much more approachable and it was easier for this group to enter into prayer with God.

When I heard William McCready, the researcher on the project, mention this I also heard him make an aside that it was interesting to note that this new group has been completely educated and formed by the post Vatican II Church whereas the older group has had a combination both pre- and post education. The image of God as Lover, Initiator of Relationship, and Wonder-full has been a consistent theme of teaching since the council within the Catholic Church.*

Mary held a very strong place among the young in this

---

* The NORC information is taken from my notes at the National Conference of Diocesan Vocation Directors at its National Convention—October, 1980 in Washington, D.C.

study. That would be considered a surprise since there has been a considerable drop of emphasis and teaching in regard to her this last decade. She holds as high a place of honor yet as she ever has in the religious imagination of the young. Religious images are passed on from one generation to the next in various and sundry ways.

The greatest influence upon the religious imagination of the young is that significant adult close to them, a mother, a father, an uncle, a very good neighbor, the parish priest, sister, or teacher. The mother stood out as the strongest influence of all significant adults.

Heaven was viewed and looked forward to as a place of wonderful delights. The delights were those fantasized as pleasurable, physical and emotional. Images related to sexuality, dancing, gaming, etc. were high in the religious imagination of heaven.

One statistic that did not seem to change with this survey was the rate of church attendance for the older young adults and the under twenty-one group. The rate of non-attendance and attendance was about the same. 40% of youth do not attend regular Sunday Mass. 70-90% occasionally miss Sunday Mass. However, the survey did reveal a different attitude. Among the older young adults there seemed to be an element of protest about not going as if they were unshouldering a burden of law. Among the younger group there was not the attitude of protest but more of an apathy, even ignorance of the importance of going. Their choice was not as aggressive or defensive as the older group. There just seemed to truly be a lack of formation in their lives of the importance of such things as regular community worship. This registers a positive note in that there really is room for education and formation in this age group. They are basically open to the good yet need to be convinced. It is a kind of "show me" attitude or openness that invites very sound, reasonable and convincing presentations.

Boys Town, in conjunction with Stanford University, has done some research work on the youth weekend retreat programs within our nation. The results were very positive and complimentary to those involved in such retreat programs as SEARCH, TEC, or other solid weekend programs. They measured a group of people before making any kind of retreat. They measured a group of same age and faith level, random sampling, coming out of a SEARCH weekend or other retreat program. Finally, they followed up these groups several years down the line in a longitudinal study. Areas such as Mass attendance and regularity were measured, attitudes about social justice, sexuality, community concerns, and family communication, as well as attitudes toward alcohol, friends, drugs, etc. were measured. Was there an immediate effect of a retreat weekend? That question was answered. Not only did something as basic as belief in God significantly increase but Mass attendance and all other areas except one improved. The one area that remained the same were the attitudes and presumptions about sexuality and its practice. Even the long range effects of the weekend proved themselves. It answered the often repeated objection that such weekends are quick fixes or temporary highs that wear thin in a hurry. There was a slight drop of the initial enthusiasm several years later but the levels of practice and belief remained higher than the general population who did not attend a retreat and higher than their own pre-retreat attitudes and practices.

Often there is the objection that such weekends are saving the saved. That did not bear up in this study. Those who were measured before the retreats did have a slightly higher profile than the general Catholic population measured. In some areas, the slight increase was not even statistically significant. The end result was that there was an increase in most areas measured after the retreat than was present before the retreat. This was the positive result.

Retreat directors of such programs everywhere welcomed this news. In their hearts they have known the good effects of such programs for years. However they have not had the research to answer the usual objections they have heard. I have found this particular piece of research most helpful when eliciting local or parish support of the retreat programs we have available in our diocese. There often is a real genuine hesitancy about such programs as to their long range merits. Plus, anything away from the home town, and new at that, always causes a little hesitancy. It is very important to instill a deep trust of the Church and speak about its sponsorship of such programs. Research adds frosting to the cake. But in the end it is the after effects, the fruit of such weekend experiences, that calms all hesitancies. Parents cannot but feel warmly towards a program that has their son or daughter loving and communicating with them more deeply than ever before.

Such positive things are happening even in subtle ways within the very spirit and attitudes of young people today. A summertime of youth work is soon to be upon us. The signs of spring are all around alerting us to be ready.

Yet, deep down, there lurks a fear among many adults, religious ministers, or potential youth workers that the soil is indeed ready, but the sower has been caught with an empty sack. What are we to plant in the new soil of positiveness, the new soil of openness to religious experience and religious conviction? How can we be convincing, convicting, and teaching? What tools are we to use for this new soil and how are we to be trained even to handle these new tools? These questions plus many more lurk in the mind of anyone embarking upon youth work and even among old timers reflecting back upon their work and continued work with youth. They are real questions deserving serious reflection. However, the fear should not be so serious or real. Braving the possibilities before us should be an anticipated experience. Understanding better what works as well as how God works allays any exaggerated anxieties we could easily pick up.

The first step was given in the previous chapter. You must be confident of the self you bring to any work or ministry. You simply bring yourself, confident of the presence and love of Christ within you and how they can come through you to others. It will not be such a big deal how untalented that self is once you arrive at a peace about your capabilities and love-ableness. Thus a youth minister will have great attention through a peaceful presence.

The second step in this business of youth ministry is a strong sense of vision—the topic of this chapter. The clearer the vision is, the better. This is the seed in the sack of the sower which is to fill the new soil. This is the seed in the sack of the sower without which the fruit of growth would be little and very scattered. By vision I would mean more than a clear sight of goals in youth work. Vision in a broad and generic way would mean more an imaginative perception of the reality of one's self, the ones you are to work with, live with, and function among, as well as an image of an outcome from the midst of youth work that would correspond to your values, ideals, faith, etc.

In establishing a vision and in attempting to reflect on that vision to make it ever more clear I believe five essential parts or ingredients would be most necessary in making up that vision of Christian ministry to young people. The first would be a deep personal faith in Jesus Christ that includes an almost equally deep communal faith in Jesus. This paints a little different picture from the individualistic faith so often extolled in evangelistic America. I as an individual cannot be separate from the communal expression of faith of those around me. At least, I will choose a community, that is, select friends and people who hold similar faith understandings and values that I hold or have been given. Yet in my life as in every individual's life there comes a time (whether a process of many years or a sudden awakening) when I must make a personal decision, a personal choice, of that Jesus my ears have heard much of. It means that I interiorize, I fully get caught up in, the spirit of Jesus alive in history and alive in me and others personally, alive in justice and love wherever I experience it, alive in ritual and prayer historically given us, alive in the serendipitous happenings of life. Jesus becomes an essential part of my consciousness in such a way that I easily move in and out of fantasy and thought concerning Him in the midst of study, meetings, shopping, working, playing. "How would the spirit of Jesus in me have me handle this?" "How would the spirit of Jesus alive in me respond to this person?" would be automatic and frequent questions contained within both the pre-conscious and consciousness itself.

Of course, this would mean most basically a beautiful love of Jesus and desire to sacrifice much for that love. For youth work can burn out many quickly unless they have the good spirituality which includes a spirit of sacrifice. And no sacrifice is possible unless there is love. A desire to be caught up in the prayer of Jesus that all be one as the Father and Jesus are one drives a worker to make oneness happen between parents and children, between spouses, between Church and individual, between young people themselves, and fundamentally first, between the Father and the world, a reconciliation done in Jesus.

One then has spiritual authority to speak when he or she knows the requirements and desires of love which includes a generous and sacrificing spirit. Where did Jesus get His spiritual authority? He first had and always had authority from the Father but subjectively people came under it when He laid down His life for them. Love consists in laying down your life for your friends as Jesus taught us. When we see that our faith in Jesus means love, and love means unity, and unity means laying down one's life, then we have spiritual authority to minister and spiritual authority that others are willing to come under or be associated with. "Laying down one's life" makes our words and actions one. No better credentials could be offered for the possibility to speak in the Lord's name.

Thus it would be most important that any and every youth minister have a place, a time, and a people where he or she can have that personal faith of theirs nurtured, replenished, and given growth in understanding and insight. It would be this same community that would replenish the creativity and ideals of a youth worker. But also, much private, quiet, personal time must be spent in reading, researching, and meditating (especially on Scripture) for replenishment to be full. Solitude is as necessary to personal faith development as the warmth of the sun is to seed growth. Not only does our faith regenerate in solitude but also our social natures regenerate. Many a time I have found that a day of solitude has taken away feelings of avoidance, fatigue, and anger in my work with people. It was as though I had a social battery that quietly and unperceived was being recharged. Faith dialogue comes easier after several hours of solitude. The natural desire to communicate erupts into dialogue with the Father and with Jesus after a good period of quiet solitude has been spent. More reflection on this will come later under point four.

The second important ingredient of a clear vision in youth work is the community practice of faith. This is distinct from the first point of having a personal faith and communal faith in Jesus Christ. Here I am writing about a community "putting into action" its common expression of faith—something that is needed both for the youth worker and for the youth that desire a deeper experience and growth in their faith life.

Today an essential element of all ministry, and especially youth ministry, is team work. Gone are the days of the "lone" retreat director or program director or prayer leader, if team is a possibility at all. A communal leadership in all these areas are most important for grand effectiveness. Plus, anyone of good faith conviction and self-possession can participate in such leadership, and youth work is available thereby to so many more. True, many yet are the leaders of youth who are dynamic and fantastic at working alone. They are special gifts of God. However, the communal witness of leadership has a power uniquely its own. As one leader said "God always works when we do it as a team." There are so many sound reasons for this.

First, the essential work of the Holy Spirit among us is UNITY. When a team is perceived as joyful and as effectively working with each other and in tune with each other—the power of unity is felt and the attractiveness of unity is strong drawing power.

Second, the teaching on the Body of Christ Paul gives to us in his writings has us appreciate the individual parts we play in the whole. The gifts we share build upon one another working together in such a way that the whole actually is greater than the sum of the parts. That is, the effect produced is greater than if each individual worked alone an equal amount of time with the exact same group, even if it is with equal enthusiasm. The Body of Christ becomes visible in team work. Scripture has it that Christ is present where two or three are gathered together in prayer. It is easy enough to state that the same Scripture supports the assertion that Christ is present where two or three are working together in His name.

It is highly practical and more ideal if the team model of youth work leadership employs a very mixed team. It is good to have some parents as part of the team, or even just one parent. It is good to see guys and gals of the youth themselves relating well to one another and leading the sharing in faith and values. In fact, the most important ingredient the youth minister needs on the team is the presence of some enthusiastic and articulate youth themselves. They usually need to be drawn from other communities, or other parishes, because of the innate fear of many people to witness to their own social peer group. This often finds youth workers in contact with each other from different communities asking for a trade of youth leader types among the young people to help them with a program or a particular evening. In any event, the Church has strongly urged the use of young people among themselves for effective evangelization.

Paragraph 72 of Pope Paul VI's declaration on evangelization *Evangelii Nuntiandi* holds forth the teaching of youth evangelizing youth, becoming actual apostles of other youth, of being sent to them to witness to faith and prayer:

> *"Circumstances invite us to make special mention of the young. Their increasing number and growing presence in society and likewise the problems assailing them should awaken in everyone the desire to offer them with zeal and intelligence the Gospel ideal as something to be known and lived. And on the other hand, young people who are well trained in faith and prayer must become more and more the apostles of youth. The Church counts greatly on their contribution, and we ourselves have often manifested our full confidence in them."*

The communal practice of faith is thus a matter that includes prayer and work, celebration and action, discipline and the constant gathering of the folks. A youth minister convinced of this often finds the new frustration being the endless phone calls and home visits to keep the team fresh and the number reliable. Yet he or she continues to work at all times to build up a team because of the conviction that the whole can accomplish more than the summation of the parts. The Body of Christ means different members and gifts working together as one.

There is an analogy that works to explain this. Picture a beautiful bonfire on a crisp Fall evening. Hours earlier the host of this bonfire extravaganza collected logs and stacked them according to what experience taught him to be the best arrangement for a maximum good burn and brilliant light. When the darkness of night is strong all are gathered around and the bonfire is begun. Hands are warmed, songs are sung, and shadows dance off the surrounding bodies keeping all huddled together more because of the eeriness of the surrounding deep darkness than for the warmth of the fire. Logs are added and the fire remains firm through the evening. Then it comes time to leave for home and the fire must be extinguished. It could burn out on its own but this would take much time. With no fire extinguisher or water handy the quickest way to accomplish this is to pull apart the logs. The one large fire is broken up into many smaller struggling flames. Easily these are put out by pitching dirt on them or by stamping feet.

The analogy is used to explain how we work together to produce the strong fire of spirit in youth work. The energy level is greater and more attracting when the logs were in flame together . . . and so it is with Christians working together in leadership. Pull them apart and leave them alone and, of course, the fire can continue in many small ways but has lost much of its energy intensiveness and attracting power. So it is with the energy to do youth work. We need to put that energy together and know the attracting and warming power therein. The same analogy works for anyone young or old who have experienced some form of conversion. They need others to keep their own new found warmth. They need others to fulfill themselves as fuel fulfills itself by being expended in fire. An individual alone does not long last nor does he or she properly expend and fulfill themselves. That is why anyone of us as Christian needs Church, why the discipline and togetherness of Church are so important for us.

This is not a quantum leap. Believing alike and praying alike is prior to working as a team. For this reason I treasure my own Catholic faith as it provides a worldwide communal oneness in ideals and prayer practice. In traveling over the world I have rejoiced in familiar prayer and communal patterns of worship. A marvelous kinship with people in general can be felt because of this. I treasure the sacramental life I enjoy. Often the wonderfulness of God is beyond any words, even of Scripture, and we need ritual to celebrate it and symbolize sublime truths and verbally inexpressible feelings. Jesus, being of men, knew this need and gave us such symbolic actions we can celebrate and participate in together.

The NORC study of religious attitudes of young Catholics revealed the desire and ready practice of ritual among youth and how our sacramental life is such a powerful fulfillment of spiritual longing and growth in the young. Any and all youth workers should not try to find a substitute for ritual or sacramental life but rather accent them, work within to improve them and orient them to youth, and then find creative additional forms of group celebrations to meet the needs of youth.

In a conversion setting such as a weekend retreat of TEC or SEARCH or something else the work of the sacrament truly comes alive. Jesus' work is manifest and vibrates energy and connections to youth. The sacrament of Penance and Reconciliation, the sacrament of Eucharist, and even the devotion and para-liturgy rituals such as benediction, renewal of baptismal promises, light ceremony, etc. convey real insights for the first time in many of the hearts of those present. What a wonderful thing to behold. It is truly a new creation when such wonderful resonance happens. Their faces beam what their hearts are feeling. We truly are a Church of God's Word *and* Sacrament. There are the expressible parts and the inexpressible parts. The mind is drawn and the heart is drawn to the mystery of God.

Thus a commitment to a Church community is a very core part of the vision of a youth director or any adult involved in youth work for they then know and can share the exigencies, growth, ups and downs, and right connections with those in their charge or contact. That commitment is as it would be to a friend—financial, emotional, attentive, time consuming, and yet rewarding. It is so helpful to see our Church community as a friend with all the responsibilities and cares and yet joys that a good friendship can bring. This leads us to the third part of this vision we each need to clearly establish within ourselves.

A few decades ago when I was a second grade CCD student, a high school senior girl was busily teaching and preparing our class one hour a week on Saturday morning to know our lessons well so that we could receive first communion at the end of the year. Upon the conclusion of the year we were handed over to the pastor of the parish for a one week summer school drill before reception of communion. Our parish priest was a seemingly stern man who frightened us as children. He had come years before from Poland by way of the concentration camps of Dachau to settle into this small rural parish. He had built up our parish church both physically and spiritually with determination and our parents had a great deal of respect for him. But we knew one thing at the beginning of our one week session—fear. How our expectation proved false. Each day was begun strictly enough, with disciplined catechism study. But as noon approached Fr. John would let up to tell stories of faith that would take us back to an imaginary Europe and to the heroes of the camps of concentration during World War II. Our eyes would fairly bug out as we would hear these stories. Then one of us would be sent downtown to bring back a box of goodies, on the parish charge account, to conclude the class. Since we had the freedom to choose we usually would bring back our favorite lunch of Pepsi, Coke, peanuts, and an assortment of candy bars.

And there were other stories, stories of first communion and saints gone by who died for the sacrament. All these story-telling sessions were really one large story of faith unfolding before us, the story of the faith of a community of faith, a Church, passed on down to another generation. Youth ministers or leaders need to have their own life stories and faith stories become one with the story of the faith community they are identified with. This is the third part of the vision of youth leadership . . . the oneness of a life story and faith story.

Often it is the case that before or after any planned youth event there is a lot of hanging around, so to speak, and the swapping of little anecdotes, memories, happenings. These are rich moments and probably more the business of youth work than anything else. How effective and powerful it is when the stories leave a point of faith within the group and it comes so naturally out of a life story or life experiences. In fact this is all in the nature of building up religious imagination within others. From there it is not a far step to challenge and see blossom creative religious imagination.

We all experience different worlds because we all receive the world through our own eyes, skin, touch, and ears. The first image we have of that which surrounds us and is within us comes through our senses. Our subconscious and conscious minds put these impulses of sight, sound, sense, hearing, feel-ing, etc. into something of a togetherness or wholeness. That is, the intellect forms a picture or image, a flash of what "it is."

Soon the same functioning mind takes many of these images and puts them together in some sensible form, some kind of patterning so that we can store it all in memory and find ways to express and repeat it. This is the foundation of imagination.

From imagination comes our ôwn unique "way of expressing" reality as we have received it, stored it, organized it, and retell it. Thus you have symbolic representation of imagination in art, music, writing, and in just plain old talk. *Religious* imagination means that the pattern of images we have stored up includes that which points to the transcendent, the beyond of things. It means images traditionally associated with faith, images of God, angels, Mary, church buildings, Bible, miracles, Christmas, Easter, etc. The richer the imagination, the more frequent and varied are the images of a religious nature. The richer the religious imagination the more frequently these images play a part in the continued perception of reality and in all retelling of that reality. Thus every story of life is influenced automatically by these religious images playing their part in the actual telling of the story.

We usually tell a story so that it contains a point of faith or a point of the transcendent in it as part of the way reality is because we have heard it told that way some time before in our lives. That is, we have listened to stories that incorporated faith in such a way which we had not realized as a possible interpretation. I think often of the harvest time when I was a child and riding along in the truck with my grandfather as we were in the fields following the combines. There would be long spells of time between hoppers full of grain and as we sat on the running board of the truck my grandfather would tell stories of his memories on the farm, going to town, and to church. It was a whole new world of the past for me and so I would urge him on to tell more stories. From them emerged a "way" of looking at things, the way he always had, it seemed. I took on some of that "way" of looking at things also when similar experiences would come into my life. My mother had a way of viewing things so that there was always that "aha" or insight of faith about all that was going on around us. I began to take on a little bit of that way of looking at things, too. And so goes growing up as we come into contact with significant others with whom we had the opportunity to spend many a story listening session. Our "slants" on interpreting and putting together reality sensibly comes from such.

We can never overemphasize or fully understand the significance of the "aha" insight of a story that has a point of faith for the imagination of young people. Good stories are retold again and again, youth to youth, youth to parent, and youth to teacher or coach. The Gospels were thusly retold generation to generation. How we cock our ears when we hear the words of Jesus, "let me tell you a story (parable)" and wait to see if we get the point. Usually there are so many points to get. It catches us where we are at regardless of age, intelligence or learning, or even cultural background, for they are common human experience stories. "There were two sons who had a dad well established. One demanded his inheritance early, the other stayed home seemingly contented. First son spent all his money on good times, went broke and was severely put upon. Coming to his senses he begs his father to take him back. The father who would normally punish severely takes him back with open arms and now second son is mad. The father loves him too but needs to celebrate the first son's return for he was lost and was found, had gone and now returned."

Even my retelling the story changed its angle and effect. The points are varied depending on if you identified with the son who went, the son who stayed, or the father. The surprise of forgiveness without bitterness is loud for all, a point of the story which everyone "gets." The story engages the heart and head.

It engages the imagination and challenges the listener to re-create and live it. So it is that a doctrine of faith, an understanding of Church teaching, or a biblical truth takes hold in the heart of youth, when, and if, it comes alive through some story lived in their lives or heard in the story of another. It is then that the "aha" of faith strikes, it is then that the heart is opened to broader truths of religion. Later we shall see how an effective youth minister employs this truth to become an effective speaker and can easily find content to talk on before any group utilizing image creation. An image is consciously and creatively drawn in speech ever larger so that it begins to incorporate many points of faith or a whole teaching.

I remember well some of the pictures of my childhood Baltimore Catechism lessons. Whatever its critical drawbacks now or even then the images associated with memorization truly did help, not only to pass tests but to capture the truth of some of the memorized facts. For instance, I remember a difficulty just listing the seven gifts of the Holy Spirit. Then after staring at this picture of a ship with seven sails it all came to me. I do not have a good memory but 25 years later I still remember the seven gifts based on that image. The front two sails were counsel and piety on the ship that was called SOUL. These braved the horizon first and rightly so, for we should not move ahead in life without these gifts. The second set of sails were the middle ones and they were three in number. They had written on them the gifts of knowledge, understanding and wisdom. For me that represented the centering force of life these three gifts were to become. Finally there were the last two sails with the gifts of fear of the Lord and fortitude. These not only took the wind first in sailing but they were largely a part of steering the course of the soul—appropriate if you think of the gifts as necessary to maintain right course in life and to even move ahead in the first place. Such a little image was not only a good mnemonic device but rich in giving me an "aha" of under-standing. A critic of this would of course say that a child is stuck with such an image and if it is a poor one then some damage could be done. However, we grow in our images and we change them readily enough if a better one comes along and captures our imagination and our understanding.

Thus images are painted in teaching, sharing, the telling of stories by which faith is learned and repeated, images by which life is tested and measured. Being conscious of how they work and their effectiveness gives the youth concerned person a powerful tool. This tool of understanding can be used for a conscious getting together of one's life story and one's faith story based on the Gospel and a rich community heritage. The way to this for each person is to know a sound and daily prayer life. This brings us to the fourth part of the vision to work with youth, and that is a personal prayer life.

At the basis of a personal prayer life is relationship . . . or relating. Thus, if God is an essential part of a person's life, then relationship with Him is as fundamental as any human friend-ship or even spousal love. It is probably more basic, or more prior. It would be most foolish to separate or split our lives in such a way that we could talk about communication with God and communication with others as two wholly separate and distinct things. As people drawn in relationship outside ourselves there is an essential relatedness between human communication and God-human communication. That does not mean there are not great amounts of understanding that can be had reflecting closely on just one of the realities. It is just that for the Christian the two always will be part of the workings of our imagination, reflection, and expression. Someone has said that in learning to communicate with God you learn to com-municate with others and vice versa for communication is communication, period.

There is a definition of prayer that shows readily how this element of personal prayer is an essential part of a vision of youth work for it is creative of the form and direction that youth work will take for any given person. That definition is offered by many contemplatives today. Prayer is seeing the connections. This is a beautiful addition to one of the traditional definitions of prayer as the lifting of one's mind and heart to God. Both require attentiveness and some quiet time. Some call this quiet time—desert time—for in order to have the time, we need the environment of solitude or isolation to guarantee the time of prayer. The desert experience is not always the geography of sand and cacti but is a matter of disciplined solitude in order to experience the wildness of God and the sense of isolation whereby surrender to God is central to survival. It is withdrawing from easily accessible stimuli and distraction of others or entertainment diversions. Why? In order to put it all together.

The images we receive from reality need the time to form up into imagination so that patterns, metaphors, even story can emerge from the collage of images. All this to come to knowledge of the connections that exist between us and the "out there" of a Transcendent God and the others of our human relationships in our work and play. The "out there" becomes then one with the "within" or inside goings on of our heart and head. In other words, we can make sense of what we are involved in at any particular point of our lives.

Youth ministry has a high burn out rate in our Church today unless the youth minister, as so often happens, moves to something in administration. The actual grass roots involvement in the lives and frustrations and growth of the youth takes its toll in a hurry unless the minister can reflect on what he or she is doing and continually see the connections of that work in the context of the larger Church-community life and in the larger context of a life story both of the self and the particular youths themselves.

Prayer is necessary to stay strong, to gain renewed energy, and not to get lost in the midst of action, movement, and heavy demands. For the frustration level is high when we rely totally on the connections of youth involvement and success in terms of numbers or solutions to particular growing up problems. Prayer takes us away from the trees far enough so that we see the forest of how there is truly a process involved in the growing up of a teenager or young adult and what incomplete part we play in that total process. We are able to reflect on our own connection or place in that overall process. It is a complete place we fill once we see the larger process of the young person's life story unfolding.

Prayer is seeing the connections. Another beautiful part of this definition of prayer is that it tells us that we do not have to create the connections. We do not have to pull out of the debris of daily living and myriad activities a unity, or force one to exist, for in God all things are connected. Thus entering into that transcendent mystery of seeing things, the connections readily begin to show themselves. Thus you have the "aha" or insight of the sense of the things you are doing. It is all related to the one source of creation and redemption and to the source of grace that sustains all. It is God who gives the increase in any work or project or even one's state of being. Therefore all things at the end of each day can and should be handed over to Him.

Seeing the connections involves our interior life as well. It can be so easy to feel disconnected at varying points in the midst of something so demanding as youth work. This is not just a phenomenon of the anxiety prone, it is typical due to the nature of the work—dealing with a volatile and mobile and maturing crowd. Disconnectedness can spell the beginning of disillusionment in work and attitude. And if there is not a source of regaining the connectedness within, then there would be no hope for gains in youth work in our Church or in youth worker numbers. Here prayer is absolutely necessary. Prayer is time and attentiveness to self and to God's love and Word. A disciplined and practiced prayer life always gives the sense of connectedness which brings all other outside relationships and activities into focus. Peace derives in large part from this "belongingness" seen through prayer. One is able to go on with renewed enthusiasm for there is much of Mary's prayer of surrender in the prayer life of the youth minister, "let it be done according to your Word."

There is so much inside the nature of youth work that requires the momentary or even long range surrender of self and work in the words "let it be." At that point we become attentive to God's grace of time at work in ways never before appreciated.

As well as the necessity of a personal prayer life in the vision of the Christian youth minister there is also delight and an advantage of having a fellow worker or friend to pray with on a regular basis. What healing and purpose there is in the prayer of two Christians attentive to the same things. I had the advantage once of having a fellow worker always wanting to pray before a road trip or project at home. They were short five minute prayer sessions of a spontaneous nature. But what a beautiful thing they did for my heart and head. Not only were they so calming but I felt God's blessings on the undertaking and a keen sense of my part in His creative-redemptive plan of things so that I knew things would unfold pretty much as they should no matter what the outcome. This was and is just one experience of the treasured statement of Jesus that where two or three gather in His name He would be present.

One final point needs to be made in this matter of the personal prayer ingredient of a vision. That point is the place and importance of Scripture as part of that personal prayer life. This is so rich that I can only serve an introduction here, which

might challenge you to deeper discoveries yourself. There are
so many ways to approach Scripture. The Catholic Tradition
deeply encourages academic study of the Word of God in such
a way that we understand how it is both the words of men and
the Word of God. Thus history, archeology, philology, critical
reflection, anthropology and many other sciences aid in the
clearer understanding of this gift to us. Any courses that can be
had in the study of Scripture would be highly encouraged in the
academic life of any youth minister, teacher, or parent. The
approach I introduce here is a little different for use in daily and
lifelong prayer. It is praying the Scriptures.

First, it is recommended that a person have a commentary
available either personally or through a parish, friend, or
school, so that troublesome passages may not be a puzzle
obstacle to prayer. It is good to frequently consult a commentary (*Jerome Biblical Commentary* is a good one) of sound
Christian and Catholic standing, especially in the beginning, in
order to get the gist of how interpretation goes within the
community of the Church. This is only by way of introduction
to the real matter of prayer.*

There is nothing like Scripture for helping to make the
connections. How often has been the time I have just picked up
the Bible and read a passage of the Gospel or Paul's letters and
it takes hold of me exactly where I am in my work or troubles or
relationships and lifts me to see my life in a different light. We
search the Word of God when we pray. But more powerful is
the fact that the Word of God searches us out both in our heart
and head. We cannot be aggressive with the Word of God. In
prayer we need to anticipate the work the Word will do in us.
For the Word is Christ and Christ speaks to our hearts. We
prepare ourselves to listen. A Trappist once helped me to pray

* Any Catholic bookstore would have many commentaries, *Barclay*, etc.

Scripture in a new and delightful way. He said one should pick up the book of God's Word with great reverence, hold it, sigh deeply over it, and pause a moment to be filled with deep anticipation and attentiveness before opening the book. The reason for this is that we need to prepare ourselves to listen to what we will read.

Many people read the Bible, but few listen to it. In fact, reading is now so common that it is difficult for us to listen to anything or anybody. When books were scarce listening was easier. Someone would read out loud and the rest would listen. The remnant of this we have left to us is that parents still read to their children. The children are still delighted. They can enjoy their own imagination as they listen to what is read. The mechanics of reading takes away some of this free play or space of imagination. Reading in itself can become a consuming process of accomplishment and therefore we do not rest in its words, images, and portrayals as we would when just listening.

Thus when we prayerfully read Scripture we need to activate our listening ability, be ready to freely leave the printed page and continue our listening in the silence and in our imagination and then restfully return to the printed word. This is ruminating. St. Bernard once said that such a person is like a cow who can chew the cud of God's Word and produce the milk of spiritual living. The Scriptures work on us slowly and more or less unconsciously. We catch things along the way almost as we catch the flu. We get the connections so to speak rather than figuring them out. The Word of God is infectious. It seeks us out.

I remember once when I was caught up in goals of prayer and Scripture reading. I would read so many pages and study so many verses of the Bible. My goal was to read the Bible once through completely each year. Thus I had to read so many pages a day. However, I was noticing that as the days went on I began to be more compulsive about the necessary amount of reading than I was concerned about listening to and praying with the Word of God. I had to drop the goal if I was to change for my days were too full to extend the time I alotted to myself. Thus I moved to a new goal of reading approximately so long, like a half hour, and let what territory I covered be totally relative. If I wanted to daydream over a verse the whole time, then so be it. What a change happened in this switch. For instance, I remember I was so troubled one day about what I was going to do next and say next. I had many irons in the fire. I began to read a psalm in the morning period I had assigned myself for Scripture. It was Psalm 46. I came upon the verse "BE STILL AND KNOW THAT I AM GOD." I was about to move on when I was grabbed within to freeze any and all reading. "Be still" was a command I had not even heard and it meant right now in my reading. So I stilled myself and vacantly stared through the chapel. I meditated. "Be still and know that I am God." Ah, I knew right then I worried too much about what I was to say and what I was to do. I was not God, I had to let God say and do more in and through my life and work. Besides that, what had to be done in my daily schedule was not God and I was not to make it God. "Be still and know that I am God, nothing else is." What a peace came over me at this time.

I listened to Scripture finally. And it searched me out where I was at and utterly healed me that day. So many other days it has done the same thing. Scripture is the Word of God and that means it is living and breathing. Living things are sensitive things. Thus the Word of God is sensitive to me and to you. It wishes to seek you out and respect you. But most of all it wishes to do you good. Therefore the Word heals, restores, refreshes and recreates. For everyone it teaches and educates and enlightens. That is its invaluableness for youth work. A ministry to the spiritual yearnings of others requires great and daily spiritual teachings.

The fifth and final ingredient I dwell on here concerning the vision of youth ministry being Christian is the simplest one to remember yet summarizes all the other parts of the vision. It is trusting that God's grace always is at work. Another way of stating this, is to say that God always works. This is the greatest preventive medicine for so-called burn out. Youth work is volatile enough and there is much natural or expected anxiety and worry along with every project planned and lived through. Will it succeed? How do you get the kids to show up? How can one compete with all the distractions of entertainment, school, friends, HBO, trips, parties, and sports? How will I handle the obnoxious, don't-want-to-be-there-but-had-to-come types? What is a good icebreaker? So the questions go through our heads and hearts, and they are right questions and need reflection and work. But they need more than dynamic answers. They need an undercurrent of trust in the youth minister that God will work and things will unfold pretty much as they should at this time.

This does not mean one cannot be as sly as a fox and as clever as the media merchants. In fact, all cleverness that can be summoned will be most helpful. Wooing, pushing, visiting, pestering and constantly working on guarantees of project and goal successes are all called for. Common working sense is required. One skit by a group of youth at a retreat recently showed me their understanding of this. The scene unfolded as if from the TV show of REAL PEOPLE. The interviewer was questioning an individual that had come to be known as the iceberg man. He was only wearing a towel in the cold Dakota winter. He claimed that he became convinced he had to learn to trust God, and so he was putting that trust to the supreme test. He gave all his clothes to the poor and now was waiting to be cared for by the Lord. He preached "Trust in the Lord with all your heart." Along came another young person and began to argue with the iceberg man. "I, too, am trusting of the Lord's love and care for me. But I know another command that says I am not to put the Lord, my God, to the test." With the help of some friends the iceberg man was taken off stage to be clothed and walk in a new and different way with the Lord, a way with much greater common sense. That made the point well that we are to trust with all our hearts but need to use our heads well to live and work intelligently.

I always have the feeling before a weekend retreat that I am entering some kind of dark tunnel for the weekend. It is as if there is something ominous awaiting me. It is a typical feeling of mine and is still there after seven years of doing weekend retreats. I don't like the feeling but have grown to live with it in such a way that I do not allow my thinking and work to be affected. I live with the mood because I know that God will work, He always has and does in ways I only learn about sometimes much later. Sunday always brings a light to that tunnel and a wide world beyond.

At one time I almost let this ominous mood-change on Friday before a retreat cause me to begin withdrawing from youth work and/or to find others to do the work. I knew after a little perseverance that this was wrong thinking. Trust was not being practiced and I was just choosing not to live with this mood. I was attempting to escape. God always works I told myself and recommitted myself to "hanging in there," to persevere. I accept now the rhythm of my moods as good companions. Their presence calls for the right and creative use of them to the advantage of those I will be loving and serving and for the glory of God. Thus they can be transformed. Thus there can be paschal mystery. Out of Good Friday comes Easter morning.

You cannot have Easter without its Good Friday. You do not fully enjoy a feast without the fasting beforehand.

The native American culture has taught us that you do not even get vision without the fasting first. Their culture had a ritual of fasting when a young person would go forth on a vision quest. In some places of the United States their culture still has this living vision quest wherein the person perceives his identity, his mission, and at-one-ness with all creation. Yet that same person perceives the suffering that awaits him in his future and he must accept that as one with creation, mission, and living.

Mary had a vision unfold for her concerning her son right from the beginning. The angel announced the extraordinariness of the child and Elizabeth confirmed that announcement when Mary was with that child. Simeon pronounced the mission of the child Jesus Mary brought to the temple and yet told Mary of her own suffering and sacrifice. Suffering and sacrifice are part of any great love. Continually each of us needs to renew our answer of affirmation to the element of sacrifice as essential part and oneness of the vision of youth ministry. Sacrifice is not easily accepted and is ever so quickly avoided even after the first acceptance. Renewal in oneself of the understanding of the requirement of sacrifice and its benefits as well as the willingness to accept it into one's soul and work takes shape through daily reflection, prayer, and meditation. The desert, prayer itself, is a sacrifice wherein all sacrifice becomes understandable. We trust in God and procede to let prayer make the connections for us. All things of our life have the chance therein to be united, at-one, and therefore peaceful. Prayer makes the connections between the story of life as it unfolds and other great stories around us, especially the greatest story of Jesus. Connections are made between faith on a personal level and on a community level so there is no separation but a unity. These stories take shape in the desert times of prayer.

The clarity of vision of youth ministry needs these elements mentioned in this chapter in order to be focused in many of the right ways on Jesus, Church, the youth themselves and on the self. These elements are not exhaustive of ingredients needed in the vision of the youth minister but seem to me to be essential to my life as a Christian leader and youth minister. They are requirements for me to keep my vision focused on the right goal of youth work—unity of people in Jesus.

"And Jesus left the crowd that had followed Him and went up to the hill country alone to pray." Never was He about to let his vision be confused or sidetracked—the reconciliation of mankind to God. He maintained the vision and its right connections to all things in prayer.

Chapter Three

THE GOOD WORD

Never let evil talk pass your lips; say only the good things men need to hear, things that will really help them. Do nothing that will sadden the Holy Spirit with whom you were sealed against the day of redemption. Get rid of all bitterness, all passion and anger, harsh words, slander, and malice of every kind. In place of these, be kind to one another, compassionate, and mutually forgiving, just as God has forgiven you in Christ.

Paul to the Ephesians 4:29-32

Not much is said anymore about mentors. In fact, it may be an almost unused term but not an unused reality. A mentor is both model and teacher. He is one who showed the way, one you wish to imitate. For a long time I had difficulty admitting that I had any real mentor, usually putting every teacher in the barrel with my parents as overall influencers of my life. However, when I get to working in a particular area of life I see myself acting or reacting as some particular person who influenced me more than others from my past.

Once I figured the most authentic way of acting was to always ask myself how Jesus would have done this, said this, or reacted to that. And it is a good, in fact, the best way of thinking and acting for a Christian. However, in reality, we usually look for a more immediate person that impresses us as the way Jesus would have acted or spoken or existed in some form today and we imitate that more specifically. We inevitably imitate that person as somewhat fitting our idea of how Jesus would have done it or said it.

It is the way we operate as human beings. We need to see flesh and blood examples of the ideas and image we have concerning Christ. It is then real for us and it is a worked out way of expression we can concretely see operating. We continually need to see Christ incarnated in our midst over and over. We need the translation of the Word of God and all its richness as well as complexities into personality, style, physical presence and ways of speaking and acting that a person embodies. Thus we are grabbed, caught up, by a person who does embody in some way the ideas and images we have developed and been taught should exist in a CHRIST-IAN, a Christ follower.

My good fortune was to be with a person who did catch my imagination both in the area of what it is to be a Christian and in the area of youth work. This was during my seminary years when I began to do youth work. The person was a priest and often directed the retreats on which I was a volunteer helper and team member. My association lasted for two years which is not a real long time, but it was a deep and varied association. I traveled with this person, vacationed with him, was intense in retreats with him and was in quiet times with him. In other words, I felt I saw him at his best and worst, under pressure and out of pressure. There was one quality that always came through which was absolute in every instance I can remember, and that was the word of support that came with his words. Sometimes there was a strange silence when I might have suspected a struggle or anger but when the talking began, over whatever matter was at hand, the positiveness of this person

came through. He had a way of magnifying the smallest remarks of a person and building on them in such a way that no
youth or older person left his presence without feeling better
about himself or herself. He was absolutely a genius at hearing
things which I never heard, from a new person, which he
would use to build up that person. An obnoxious teenager was
just a welcomed challenge on a weekend to melt with love and
support. And it was not just the young retreatant. The team felt
it, too, right in the process of work together, even if at times not
consciously perceived.

Now that was Christ-like to me. That is what I wanted to be
able to do. But I knew that before I could do it, I had to be it. I
had to look closely at how Paul's words on being Christ-like in
speech ("say only the good things men need to hear, things that
will really build them up") really was an authentic part of this
person and not just an effective technique. I knew that it had to
captivate my thinking, my habits, my consciousness and my
unconsciousness. I knew that it had to just flow out of my pores
so that in good times and bad times such speech would be
readily available. I saw such speech as the most effective
building of the body of Christ I had yet witnessed in my life. And
so I began to meditate on those words of St. Paul. And now,
years later, I still meditate on those words hoping they will
possess me totally.

This was just one strong example in my life of an imitation I
deemed worthy to admit in my writing and speaking. I had a
true mentor. He made something Christ-like take on personality and flesh. He demonstrated that such Christ-like qualities
recommended in Scripture is more than just a nice ideal but
can be real. It gives life, life with gusto, that the Kingdom of God
should have.

But this example is based on something deeper that happens to every human being or is, at least, the desire and longing

of every person. That too was captured by John the Evangelist in his writing when he wrote down under inspiration that Love consists not in the fact that we love but that God has first loved us. Psychology makes millions 2000 years later telling us that we cannot give what we don't first have. We give because we first have received and that is a secret of the human sciences as well as theological sciences shared popularly everywhere. Yet we all need to grasp so much more of this truth if not the original meaning for the first time in our individual lives. That longing of every person is the full felt knowledge that we have actually been loved first.

One might come up with a number of different ways of expressing this reality of our desire to be first loved. However, there is a meditation on Jesus and His Father that serves well for the youth worker though it can be generalized to everyone as it is true of everyone. In the New Testament we frequently witness Jesus in prayer with His Father. He shares some of the intimacy of that communication, the greatest being the very personal and family title "Abba" (daddy) with whom Jesus communed. "Father, take care of these little ones" "Father, your will be done" or "The Father and I are one." He shared the fatherhood He knew with all of us when He taught us to pray together "Our Father in heaven. . . ." He knew that we had to have a father and that we too need to be intimate with a father.

We know from the reality of Scriptures that Jesus became one of us. And one of us means knowing all the needs and growth that are part of our lives. Being "fathered" is one of those basic requisites of being human. Jesus had that deep sense of being "fathered"—loved and nourished into existence as one of us by a Father, though divinely He always existed as one with the Father. He shared that deep sense of fatherhood with us, and invited us to know how we have been "fathered."

And so I look deeply at how I have been loved first and nourished with life. I recognize the ways I have been fathered in my birth, in my childhood, in my schooling, and in my adult life.

So many people today have not experienced yet that reality of being fathered. Maybe "dads" aren't being real "dads" in our culture or maybe these people have not allowed themselves to be fathered. Or maybe the tragedy of family breakups and high mobility have not provided the chance of fatherhood. Yet we will never grow up, become mature adults, unless somewhere along the line we have been properly "fathered"—loved and nourished into existence by someone powerful in our lives. We have to humanly know that so that spiritual fatherhood has real meaning and possibility.

Obviously there has been physical fatherhood and motherhood in our lives. But here we refer to the fatherhood and motherhood of the human spirit that is so much more involved than the physical conception of a human being. It calls forth what is most human in us—the transferral of life and love, the spirit of thought, of will, of meaning and purpose to another human being. In other words we are humanly loved and nourished into existence by a "father" or a "mother." Now sometimes that requires influence of the human community, or members within the human community, different than the actual physical mother or father. That is why we as members of the Body of Christ are responsible to "father" and to "mother" others—to give spiritual birth to their humanity. Yet we cannot "father" another or "mother" another until we have been "fathered" or "mothered" ourselves in some spiritual and emotional sense. That is the whole point for the youth worker. He or she could not be helpful to the life and spirit of a young person unless he or she possessed the sense of being "fathered" and "mothered" himself or herself. When a young worker recognizes another reaching out to him or to her for this very important need, it is well to know that need or longing of the heart to be "fathered" or "mothered." Yet that youth worker must seriously examine himself or herself to know that in "fathering" or "mothering," that person eventually is set free—free in order to themselves "father" and "mother" their peers, their own parents, or those younger than themselves.

Jesus spoke to us that His authority was from the Father and that what we would see and hear of Jesus would be from the Father. Jesus told us His life was from the Father. Thus, the spiritual fatherhood that Jesus showed to us is to be a part of all of our lives. It is a powerful part of living, and leads in turn to being a father or a mother oneself. That kind of sense of fatherhood in our lives, that sense of unity under a father as brothers and sisters, can threaten the world that feels insecure, that has not known the depth of fatherhood or motherhood. But yet it is so attractive. In fact, it is irresistibly attractive to others. A friend of mine, who loves to pray Scripture, has said that there are really only three great prayers of the New Testament and "Father" is one of them. These prayers are *Come, Jesus,* and *Father.*

There is so much meaning to the advice of St. Paul to say only the good things people need to hear, things that will really build them up. Another one of those meanings is how the support of love works in actually changing a person's life. There is a common saying within communication workshops between couples that it is easier to love a person into new ways of acting than to drive them into new ways of acting. Basically what this means is that we have to accept the other person exactly where they are at, and who they are, that very moment in time. Jesus is in that person and present to that person exactly as they are right here and right now. So in a sense we do not really expect change. We just love that person and miracle of miracles, change begins to happen. It is so hard not to expect change, or not to very subtly manipulate a person into the kind of behavior that we would like to see coming from that person. (This does not mean that we cannot demand respect for our own persons or allow nothing other than respect or that we cannot act to maintain good order in relationships. This is very much a way of loving and creating an environment wherein greater loving can take place).

This is why it is good for a couple even when they are preparing for marriage, and are engaged, to ask themselves if they could accept that person whom they love just as he or she is at this moment in time without having a hidden agenda of how that person will change after marriage. I am afraid many couples would not choose marriage at such an early date in their dating lives if they had the sense of loving that person exactly as they are here and now without expecting change. Yet that does not mean we do not trust that change will happen or can happen. We do know that if a person is "fathered" or "mothered" correctly, and is first loved, then they can love in return. We do believe that then the other will want to change and will actually continue to grow.

Change runs behind the heart. By that I mean once the heart knows and feels the change it wants to make in life, the actual behavior comes in a catch up fashion. In fact, it seems among adults where I witnessed a conversion of heart there is about a two year lag before the conversion of speech and act comes full swing. Thus it is so important to continue to bathe one another in love and support. For often such a person will otherwise get easily discouraged at the slow progress, or seemingly impossible life changes of habits and personality, he or she now so desperately is making. Thus the only expectations we have of one another are of ourselves that we will continue to love, forgive, support, and speak good things at all times.

Saying only the good things others need to hear, things that will really build them up requires positive thinking, positive attitude, and positive speech as a matter of habit. The habit and the practice comes from both this deeper conviction that the Body of Christ is built by positive, supportive relating, by first loving, by "fathering" and "mothering" another so they can in turn do the same but also because it is fundamental to being a Christian. By that I mean that we are to see in each person the presence of the divine, the presence of Jesus. Mother Teresa of Calcutta made this known worldwide. How could she handle the dying people eaten up by worms and disease and treat them as if each person had been the only child of a mother? Because she truly does see Jesus in each person. She is ministering to Jesus and to Jesus' loved one in each instance. This is a marvelous instance of the combination of divine and human love.

One aspect of divine love is that, as the Bible states, we are each called by name. God knows us and calls us by name into existence. It is likewise one of the great human acts of love we can become practiced at. We are thrilled when a new acquaintance remembers our name. It builds us up inside, especially when we are called by name out of a crowd of new names. We are a somebody at that moment. It is one of the great acts of love in youth work.

Now not everyone is so gifted at names so as to remember everybody they meet. I definitely am not one of those gifted ones. Hubert Humphrey was supposedly famous for remembering names of people he met at dinners, gatherings, etc. I had a friend who was called by name by Senator Humphrey at a dinner for the handicapped a year after they had only casually met in some other circumstance. There are very few people like that. Yet we can all greatly improve our own skill in that area as an act of love for others.

I once had a professor in college who walked in the first day of class and greeted all the new students. He walked in our midst and alphabetically called off the names from a class roster he had memorized. He took a few moments to match the face with the name and went on. He would do this the first two classes and after that we were all known and called on by name. Obviously he was a favorite among students. His teaching material was not that outstanding, but I only see this now, for at the time everything he taught had a special quality about it because each one of us mattered to him. Likewise, he stood in sharp contrast to the typical college professorial style of lecturing and testing impersonally where the only concern for the name would be the final grade, that it matched correctly the given name on the original roster. I was so impressed by all this that when I began to teach in a high school myself several years later I worked hard a week before the semester began to memorize every name I was to have in class. I discovered there was a power in readily and immediately calling a person by name, some of it in discipline, but more of it in love. Class material was somewhat of a breeze after that.

Sometimes on retreats I like to challenge fellow team members to catch every name as new SEARCHers or TECites introduce themselves. Always there is someone from the team members who can call each person by name if the group is not too large. Of course, it is impressive but it shows how concentration can improve this skill for everyone.

Recently at one retreat new people began to introduce themselves. I was half listening and thinking of all the plans and activities that had to come off for the weekend. After the first three sat down, having just introduced themselves, I tried to recall their names. I could not. That made me quite angry at myself for not loving these people enough to at least try. Then and there I resolved that I would know every person by first name (all ninety people) before the finish of the weekend. I eliminated everything else from my mind—those before me were all that mattered in the world. It became relatively easy to learn all the names that weekend for I had most of the names down by the end of the introduction itself.

It was so easy to get caught up in myself and plans thinking this was loving during the weekend. And I was ignoring an act of love right under my nose. I was being called to be attentive and listening to those present; for the weekend had begun and nothing other really mattered than the right here and right now of those young people. This was part of their first act of invest-ment of themselves in the weekend and I better honor that, build on that, compliment that by a total attentiveness on my part.

There are so many other ways of saying the good word, things that will really build people up. Always we are to look for the gifts God has granted each individual. It should be a personal challenge to uncover those gifts in the new person we meet. One of the hard things I had to learn in being a Christian man was that another person's gain was not my loss. It was hard for me (and I think men in general) to readily compliment and praise others. But for the Christian another person's gain, another person's upbuilding, is not my loss but is my gain. That attitude had to start with my own companions and fellow workers with whom I so easily felt competitive. Women have often showed me the way in this for they usually practice praising more easily than men. They have taught me how such is an act of love. At least, there were several women in my life who were especially loving in this way to people they met.

Before complimenting it is necessary to first listen well. You take in everything that you can and then gently you can men-tion something they said or something you noticed that will be a form of praise or support. There are the physical compliments on the smile, eyes, hair of the other. We are undivided spiritual-physical realities, and we enjoy compliments about any part of the creation that is us. Young people are especially sensitive to all their new physical growth and how they physically present themselves. So many think they resemble a version of the elephant man or woman as they enter the room until these suspicions are completely put to rest. Thus observation of an athletic skill or bearing is very upbuilding. A comment on how a person is dressed, their taste in good fit or appearance, is commentary on the physical nature of the other person. An interest or hobby will come out in conversation with anyone and it is so easy to pick up on that interest and listen it right into a compliment for the other person. Attentiveness to a detail dropped here or there on which we build immediately compliments another in a tremendous way. The other's gain in a sense of self worth, confidence, and positive self-thinking is the world's gain and the gain of the Body of Christ.

How beautiful are those that bring good news to the world in the good they can say about others. They shall bring happiness to themselves and to countless others.

Chapter Four

THE MUSIC BEHIND THE WORDS

Parents and Children—Encourage one another: Picture yourself as a large hypodermic needle injecting the serum of courage into the veins of those whom you speak a cheerful word. Think of the badly behaved people as discouraged people, allergic to the poison of rejection, and therefore pessimistic that anyone else will appreciate or even recognize their useful, loving contributions to society. Dennis L. Gibson Ph.D.

Today's parents expect to make fewer sacrifices for their children than parents did in the past, but they also demand less from their offspring in the form of future obligation than their parents demanded from them. Yankelovich Survey

About the Truth: Discipline your children while they are young enough to learn. If you don't you are helping them destroy themselves. Proverbs 19:18

Yet children produce parents, too: "Who of us is mature enough for offspring before offspring themselves arrive? The value of marriage is not that adults produce children but that children produce parents." Peter DeVries

Dear God, The People in the next apartment fight real loud all the time. You should only let very good friends get married. Child's Letters to God

"The people who experienced the most punishment as teen-

agers have a rate of wife-beating and husband-beating that is four times greater than those whose parents did not hit them." This study also found a close tie between violence and the method a couple uses for making decisions. If the husband makes almost all decisions, he is far more likely to hit his wife or be hit by her. Between husbands and wives who share the decision making, there is almost no violence.

Murray A. Straus, Richard Gelles, Suzanne K. Steinmetz

"Dr. Peale, what advice would you give a young couple who are considering the idea of having no children at all in their marriage?" "I would tell them that it is a very great mistake, that the purpose of marriage is to have children, to procreate and repopulate the earth. This is God's method for keeping the human race going. I think it's a denial of God's sacred plan not to have any children, to say nothing of the fact that this will eliminate a vast amount of happiness from their lives."

Dr. Norman Vincent Peale

Often youth workers relate to youth apart from a family context, in a group with other youths, and can easily forget that each individual young person brings not a lone identity, or an independent identity, as it so often might seem. He or she brings with himself or herself the identity of the whole family that she or he comes from. One needs to be aware when addressing youth that we are speaking to a much larger audience than is present and we are speaking to a people who have not sorted out their history and their individual part in that history. Nor have they sorted out a sense of self, measured

---

*These gems were taken from a pamphlet called *Family Concern*, published monthly as part of Youth for Christ/USA P.O. Box 419, Wheaton, Illinois 60187.

against the larger world, apart from their own individual families. Attitudes, expectations, and many questions remain just below the surface.

The young person's life comes from the family environment. In a certain sense it is as if the young person before you has been programmed to act out, to say, and to feel certain things they do not even know the source from which such things come. Yet there is a desire, and this is where freedom comes into play, to test all parts of our individual history against a larger sense of what life is, to seek out values and ideals whether they were a part of our family or not.

The title of this chapter derives from a story I heard once that can demonstrate how parents and family, by their expectations, shape the thinking and desires of a child growing up. It is a small story about vocation awareness within family life. It was related once by a mother who had a six year old daughter who began a school where sisters taught. One day, about two months into the school year, the daughter came home. She came bouncing in through the front door ready to visit with her mom as she usually did after school. Mom was busy baking cookies and had her arms full of dough almost to the elbows and the little girl asked her mother whether she ever thought about what she was going to be when she grew up even as early as the first grade. Well, mom replied that she supposed she had had dreams and thoughts about this and wondered what little Ann was thinking about. Ann said that she had been thinking about growing up, getting married, and having ten children.

Mom decided to play a little bit with that idea and joked with Ann and told her that when the time came and this happened she would have to plan on building a big house so that when grandpa and grandma came over to their house there would be a big enough room for one table with all the grandchildren around it so that "we can pray and we can visit about all the little tricks you did when you were a small girl." That day the conversation ended with some giggles and what kind of children those ten would be like.

Several months later Ann came home from school. She bounced into the front door and was all concerned about visiting on growing up again. She said, "Mom, is it okay to change your mind about what you are going to be when you grow up?" Mom said, "of course it is." "I have been thinking," said Ann, "I have been thinking that when I grow up I don't want to get married, I think I will become a sister and get married to Jesus, and then all the children in the world will be my children." Mom later said that she did not realize how quick her response was or what it meant. But her response was, "Honey, you're much too young to be thinking about that now." As the years went by Ann grew up and never once did she mention this desire which seemed so strong at one time as a first grader. In later gained wisdom, mom realized how her conversation in her daughter's life really did shape the different kinds of hopes and dreams she had when she was growing up. Children really are concerned about the expectations of their parents and without realizing it often do live out those expectations in some way or another.

The music behind the words in this instance was clear. Mom was saying it was great to think about the life of being married and having a big family. In the second instance mom was saying basically that she was scared. Her daughter was thinking about the sisterhood and mom did not really want to talk about it. It is the music behind the words that children are keen at picking up and planting in their hearts.

The attitudes, convictions, values and ideals are the true music behind the words in a young person's life. Even the words of anger or protest or rebellion, even the acting out on the drug scene, or vandalism, or running away are instances of the deeper musical happening in the person's life. That musical may be a cry for help or a cry for consistency or a cry to the world to show itself in some person as real, as good, as authentic and honest, as well as strong. There are probably much larger concepts than the example given above concerning a vocation that shape the musical in a person's life, like the whole nature of how we perceive ourselves, our sexuality, our talents, our own goodness, and our possibilities for the future. Even our consciousness of a greater Reality that determines things in life, to which we are all oriented, is part of the melody weaved through the music of our lives.

Being interested in the history of the young person's life helps to minister to that person. It alerts us to listen to what lies behind the appearance or impression created by that person. Many things and many persons have contributed to the creation of that history, that musical of his or her life. We are just one more person along that path, but maybe a crucial one if it is God's choosing.

This awareness of the kind of history wrapped up in the young person makes the work of the youth minister more insightful, more understanding. It does not really change the love, care, or sense of responsibility the youth-concerned person would have. Always it gives the youth minister or worker the greater sense of need and receptivity in the young person for a good word, a word of praise and support, a word to build them up.

A word may be spoken in praise of someone's good looks, smile, clothes, etc. This actually enhances the person's self appreciation in the area of sexuality. Of course, sexuality is so much broader a reality than the mere sex of a person or the societal sense of sexi-ness. Sexuality is inclusive of personality, maleness, femaleness, what it means to be a man or a woman in the world today, what is essentially common to all humans regardless of maleness and femaleness, physical attributes, communication between men and men, women and women, and men and women, a sense of what intimacy is all about, and finally, what it means to be a mother or a father in the world today. This last point is often overlooked. The sense of what it means to be a mom or dad relates to sex life, communication, responsibility, and family life. That sense is first gotten, and in some way held forever, by what our own individual moms and dads were to us—how they fathered us or mothered us. Sexual education begins when you are first born a boy baby or a girl baby. Instantly a whole way of reacting to you begins between mom and dad and you.

Many problems in family life or the life of an adolescent relates back to the way mom and dad treated that person as boy baby or girl baby. Likewise, another whole area of what it means to be man or woman in the family and the world is picked up as music behind the words and acts of parents in the way they, mom and dad, treat each other and love each other. These are called essential relationships. From them comes a way of relating. The mere emergence into adolescence will not change that even if the desire to do so is strong. That is why you may be an important path to that change by the style of relating you portray and by the demonstration of relationships in teamwork that you work and live.

This morning I had a youth team leader in my office telling about a high school one-day-retreat they had completed. He was a little down as he related how so many of them are such good kids but seem unable to establish a relationship to the Lord. What could they say to the kids that would turn them. I know the team to be talented. The only advice I could think of giving was to continue on the course they had planned (they planned to travel to many locations during an interim break in college). More important than what they said, the music they sang, or the jokes they told, was that they continue doing what they were doing, and do it as a team. Young people will pick up on the music behind their performances and see how they relate to and love one another. They will hear what they really value in their hearts no matter what is said or done. That will have the profound effect that good Christian community always has had from the Acts of the Apostles onward. Thus it would be best that they share frequently themselves about what their faith is and be sure they are in tune to each other and to the Lord. That will produce an irresistible harmony. Besides, the young people will need time in their own lives to come to such relationships. Everything goes together. As they can relate more healthily and joyfully with their friends, as they can relate better with their families, and as they can relate more wholesomely with a boy friend or girl friend, then they can relate more deeply with the Lord. Immediate results can never be sought, expected, or even seen as natural. When the unnatural happens where there is a turnaround or great change, praise God for his blessing.

The goal of relationship with each other and with the Lord is intimacy. It is the way of engaging another or relating that we deeply desire. Intimacy is the ability or capacity to commit oneself to particular individuals in our lives. The easier first step of loving all humanity ("I love people") is followed with the more difficult second step of growth to love this friend, this mom or this dad, or this teacher that I am stuck with.

There is a maturity scale those who have studied human behavior have proposed to us that naturally takes place in a young person's life if given the right support and environment for it to happen. It is called the growth stages of dependence and independence.

The first stage is dependence wherein a child is automatically stationed. That child begins, almost immediately, experimentations in independence (testing mom or dad or the baby sitter). These experimentations grow and recede until the time of adolescence which is the second stage of development.

Here we see a person move from dependence to a counter dependence. There is no real independence yet, but rather, internal struggles with authority persons or institutions he or she had been or still is dependent upon.

Frequently some people become arrested at this stage of development and maturity and do not even move on to the internally desired third stage of self-dependence or independence. This stage is not only freedom from the former dependence the individual had but in its positive sense is a freedom of doing things on one's own initiative. It is a time of enough self-possession to actively be responsible for the good that can happen in the world and for self support. This requires skills of living and making a living but more importantly it requires an attitude of self knowledge and self confidence and self responsibility so that the circumstances of our surroundings do not determine solely whether I can be independent or not. It is the sense of pulling my own weight now and being presently one of the caretakers of the world or society such that I can now not only take care of myself but will answer for my own decisions.

This third stage can begin to happen in childhood and yet be mingled with the dependence that is still necessary for growing up and protection and education and nourishment, etc. As it can be present early in development it can be absent from a person's life throughout that life if they have not grown or matured. The more likely happening in our society is that this becomes the last struggle of development. We live in a highly individualistic society where rugged independence is fostered and encouraged. "Going it" alone is a common artistic portrayal in movies and novels. Taking on the world alone and winning is our image of the heroic.

Yet this is not the end of maturity nor is this the way encouraged by Jesus or the early Christian community. The way encouraged actually is the fourth stage of growth called interdependence. It is the humbling realization that I cannot go it alone and that I choose not to do so in any event. "I need others" becomes the realization of this stage of growth. The positive side is that I am needed by others and that I make a huge difference to the whole and that I can choose the group whom I will be interdependent with. That means I can choose a friendship and partnership of believers and give my all to that group and do all I can to love them and increase their unity.

Unity becomes an overriding value and concern. Within that I can master the art of compromise or develop the art of sharing. I cannot only live with others but I can work with others and even change my habit of doing things for the sake of unity. The negative side of this whole stage is that I realize how weak I am. I might never have established the third stage of my growth in independence and thus I am more dependent than inter-dependent. I hang on others and take more than I give. Or I must have my way in things for I am trying to meet my independence needs in the midst of a group that requires inter-dependence.

Though these four stages seem like clean break-ups of growth pattern they are so only in theory. In actuality they overlap and move in varying ways of complexity at the same time, especially from adolescence through to the end of life. Awareness of this inner working of growing up helps the youth director both respect what is happening to the young person and also shows the director or minister what that young person can be called to as she or he grows. The fourth stage means arriving at a kind of Christian charity or altruism about living together in a true brotherhood or a true sisterhood of human beings. This first happens in and among family members, then friends, with authority figures, and all others we work with or are in contact with in some form or another.

These stages of growth are unto intimacy and the full flowering of sexuality in a person's life. The fourth state of interdependence leads one to be able to experience intimacy in its proper perspective and depth, as well as in its Christian sense. This state not only brings about a better understanding of what sexuality is all about but encourages it to be lived in a wonderful form of freedom.

Sexuality is seen as wonderful by the Church. There are several parts of our faith that accent its wonderfulness. We believe Jesus became one of us in the flesh. That is the incarnation. He anointed us as physical creations in that moment. He related sexually then to the world and others when on earth, that is, as a man with words, looks, actions, and gestures. He showed us that we are all a part of the new creation in Him. He showed us a way of relating to the creation of His Father, both the physical world and the human world. He showed us a way of relating to the transcendent world—to the Father, and He invited us to a unity of relationship with Him in all relating.

The Church has always held to its beliefs and even developed its beliefs and values by way of "shared wisdom" of the believers and their leaders. It is the pattern to be followed in education in sexuality. What we learn of our sexuality and how we grow in it is as much a community affair as it is a home or private affair. If the Church teaching could be summarized by way of some theological principles it would probably take the form of the following principles developed through the United

States Catholic Conference.* They can well form the foundation for a Christian description of human sexuality.

1) Each person is created unique in the image of God.

2) Despite original sin, all human life in its physical, psychological and spiritual dimensions is fundamentally good.

3) Each person is created to be loved and to love, as Christ, loved by the Father, loves us.

4) Human relationships are expressed in a way that is enfleshed and sexed.

5) Human sexuality carries the responsibility to work toward Christian sexual maturity.

6) Mature Christian sexuality, in whatever state of life, demands a life-enriching commitment to other persons and the community.

7) Conjugal sexuality is an expression of the faithful, life-enriching love of husband and wife and is ordained toward the loving procreation of new life.

These are principles. They are never that cleanly taught in the home, Church, or the school. No matter how clear the principles are it is still true that a young person receives formation in the area of sexuality more by what is caught than is taught. Psychosexual development begins with the first human contact and continues in and through every other human contact throughout the years of life as we grow from an immature self-centeredness to mature Christian altruism and generosity—the fourth stage of development called interdependence. Thus the words of Scripture come alive "see how they love one another."

*Education in Human Sexuality for Christians: Guidelines for discussion and Planning. USCC, 1312 Mass. Ave. NW. Wash. D.C. 20005. Catalogue # 691.

Another characteristic tune going on in the young person's life is that of idealism. Many developmental people say that this hits hardest and blossoms forcefully in the junior high years but it never really seems to wane until one is into his or her twenties or even thirty years old. What a power in human living this is. Idealism is what propels us into the world and tests our talents, gifts, and independence in a good sense. It challenges the whole world to deliver its best. The challenge to adults is eminently clear, to be authentic through and through. Of course, many youth easily succumb to cult type of groups which promise a kind of utopia and capitalize on the ready idealism of the young. This would be the more negative side of this marvelous power in human living.

Youth workers should expect idealism, be ready to help develop it as a natural part of the lives of youth, and know how to tap into this great resource. They should likewise be wise in the attractive power of fundamental groups, who demand all in the leaving of family, money, and possessions, to young people. Young people need to be wisely and gently reminded of this possibility in their lives. But the fact of some following cult type of groups reminds us to know the challenge we can give, the high expectations we can put forth. They are looking for something very heroic, not only to follow but also to be a part of themselves. They are after a more inclusive reality than just an idea; they are after a whole life style. The reason for this should be clear. Young people are not able to know what all the detailed decisions should be in their lives in following out a value or belief. They want to be shown, guided, and even pushed to form a way of living that is all inclusive and consistent with their values, ideals, and has a great chance of the heroic.

Militaries around the world have known this since wars began. The young person is the best to recruit not just for physical vigor but because of the idealism present waiting to be channeled. Thus it was not only a temptation in modern times but has always been a reality that a country embattled will move younger and younger into the teen years for combatants rather than up into the twenties and thirties. This is so even when professional sports have shown that physical vigor can well last late into the thirties, a kind of vigor militaries require for combat.

The only recorded instance we have in the Scriptures of Jesus as a youth is in the Gospel of Luke where we have the report of His trip to Jerusalem with His parents and fellow travelers on an annual pilgrimage to the Holy City. His parents discovered enroute home that their son was not with them and began to worry. They returned to Jerusalem and found Him teaching in the temple impressing even the doctors of doctrine. His response to the worried remarks of His parents, coming as a kind of chiding, was that He had to be about His Father's business. He went home with them and grew in wisdom and age. Jesus' estimated age was twelve.

This is not exactly a lesson in parental obedience though it can allow for a teaching there. It is a demonstration of Jesus' emerging awareness of His mission from the Father. It is a story about idealism as well. Here we have a story about a person who became man as us and even was young as us, emerging into His teen years with hopes, plans, answers, and some independence. The point of idealism is this. Jesus was ready to begin His Father's work at that age, which seemed like a tremendous responsibility. But He went home and breathed maturity into that idealism of His faith both received and acquired. It is an instance of this idealism being channeled.

Thus the youth worker taps the idealism of the young person but is prepared to channel it, to give it wisdom, age and grace. The youth minister can do this in many ways. Young people with high expectations may find in the youth worker some ideal (even something the youth worker is unaware of) that makes their own idealism seem possible. Remember, the young person is measuring his or her idealism against the real to see what is possible. A youth worker may well be that possibility of the real they are in some way looking for in another. When I was in grade school and junior high I remember the ones I really kept my eye on were some of the neighborhood single guys that were now out of school and living their independence in some way. How they did that, and their attitude about life, etc. were important to me. And I am sure that when I came to be that age of finally being out of school or having a good independent summer job I did not think or realize how there were younger guys studying and looking at me. In any event, there is much to appreciate and channel in the idealism of youth. Rally it for the cause of community building and for more authentic Christianity within the Church community.

The word "parenting" has often been used to indicate some of the realities this chapter has spoken about when saying "fathering" or "mothering." Whatever terminology is employed, though I chose "fathering" and "mothering" as a richer image for the Christian family, developmental psychology offers a rich wisdom in regard to the discipline that should undermine or form the basis of all teaching, loving and sharing between parents and children. This applies to the youth worker in that he or she is caught up into a form of parenting as well. It also becomes important to the youth worker for that person is often asked advice concerning discipline of children or the raising of children. I suffered a good amount of anxiety over discipline situations that might arise when I was conducting classes or gatherings with youth. There are two words or realities to remember as a distillation and summary of much of developmental psychology: *consistency* and *definite limits*.

There are many debates in the area of parenting concerning the discipline and the raising of children. One instance may be the appropriate mode of punishment a parent should give a wrongdoing. An old cliché honors one side of the debate that the punishment should fit the crime and that if the physical is called for, the swat or spanking should be low enough, soon enough, and convincingly enough. Others quickly protest any form of corporal punishment towards children, regardless of age, as something disposing a child toward violent tendencies and causing doubt to arise in the child's life about parental love. It is better to reason with the child so that when he or she becomes a teenager you can continue in a way of operation that has been natural to family communication all along. The other side will counter that words are not enough and that something symbolic of the deep commitment of the parent to right behavior must be demonstrated. If this is not a spanking when the child is young, then a form of restriction of freedom, or something very much felt and not just heard in the child's life, is necessary to instill the inner discipline a child needs to develop.

There are debates about how to set curfews or how to treat one child different from another child if serious problems arise. There are opinions on how and when dating should take place, early in the teen years or mid-teen years. Another area is the use of the family car or the purchase of a personal car. Always lively in the family setting is the judgment over allowance and corresponding responsibilities. This ties in with whether an outside job should be sought in light of the pressure of education on the young person's life or whether some just compensation should be given to the son or daughter if they decide to dedicate their time more to studies and family life.

Whatever the discussion, I have discovered that there is a

simple wisdom by which to find solutions and answers to the many varying issues. That is to remember always to be consistent from one age to another, from one child to another, from one issue to another, and to always set definite limits about what will be tolerated. And always be willing and ready to back up these limits with a commitment of time, discipline, love and sacrifice.

Thus it matters less what type of punishment is used on a small child (traditional, reasonable, etc.) in love than that the parents are consistent with each other and with their child from one matter to the next. Anxious trauma is produced in a person growing up if they do not know what to expect of their parents or to expect two totally different things of their separate parents. Manipulation is quickly mastered by the child who can play off the inconsistencies of one parent versus the other parent or of past offenses treated differently though the offenses were of a similar nature.

In the end it will make little difference between the outcome of maturity of young people in one family that has lighter limits and those with very strict rules as long as internally each family is consistent with some definite limits of toleration. *Consistency* of particular parenting and *definite limits*, clearly understood by all within the family setting, are not a guarantee in the modern world of beautiful maturity of a child but they are two of the most fundamental requisites for healthy growth in a child that I have studied, observed, and experienced. They are necessary to inform the love of mother and father towards proper expression in order to get at the end result desired in the love parents have for their children.

Sometimes love is tender love, and at other times love needs to be tough love, but it is not any less a Christian love. Parents can never be swallowed up in their desire to protect their children from any pain and suffering, or being overly zealous to have them perfectly happy or contented. Sacrifice and discipline is a part of the reality of living and especially of Christian living. It is part of the Paschal mystery. In that we believe there can be no Easter Sunday without a Good Friday. There can be no feast without a fast of some kind. To know the resurrection joy of Christian living we must know the Good Friday sorrow of dying to oneself.

The first letter of John (chapter 1) expresses well the desire which parents and youth workers alike have in sharing the good things of life in the Lord with others, especially those most precious to them. It expresses well the music behind the words of love that would "father" or "mother" another. "What we have seen and heard we proclaim in turn to you so that you may share life with us" (Summary: 1 Jn 1).

The final piece of knowledge a youth worker should have in working with youth, but especially with their parents, is how to handle the guilt of mom or dad when things have gone wrong. Constantly parents need to be reminded and assured that their child is a separate human being and has a unique and powerful freedom of his or her own. That is often a hard reality to accept. Those who are close to us (not just children, but friends as well) somehow involve us in wanting to control or influence as completely as possible their freedom towards the good. We cannot always know all the influences upon that freedom no matter how close we are to the person or how well we think we know them. Life is just too complex to assume that kind of knowledge. This allows withholding judgment of individuals even if we are outraged at their behavior because we respect the mystery of the inner workings and exterior influences upon a person. It is a wonderful, freeing thing to leave that final judgment in God's hands. Thus we just love kindly, patiently, toughly, and perseveringly.

Chapter Five

SEARCHING . . . AND GETTING AWAY

THE STRANGER THAT I WAS

LORD, tonight I ask you, once and for all, to
    rid me of my concern
    over what impression I make on other people.
Forgive me for being so preoccupied
    with what I seem to be,
    with the effect I produce,
    with what others think and say of me.
Forgive me
    for wanting to imitate others to the extent that
    I forget who I am,
    for envying their talents so much that
    I neglect my own.
Forgive me
    for the time I spend playing games with my "personality"
    and for the time I don't spend in developing my character.*

* From the *Notre Dame Prayerbook for Students*, Ave Maria Press, 1975.

St. Angela Merici, who lived in Italy in the 1500's, and
worked with young girls, especially those who were im-
poverished in some way, wrote words of wisdom to her fellow
teachers. "God has given free will to everyone, and therefore
he forces no one but only indicates, calls, persuades. Sometimes, though, something will have to be done with a stronger
command. But always bear them, so to speak, engraved upon
your heart—not merely their names, but their conditions and
states, whatever they may be."

The great teachers of our faith have always respected the
great mystery of freedom present in every individual as a true
gift of God. And because of that gift of freedom in every young
person, no matter how we love them and direct them and
convince them, the searching goes on in their lives. The searching is a part of their continual testing of reality and checking the
limits and authenticity of those things they encounter in order
to check their ideals against reality and to learn the extent of
their own limits in the areas of talents, gifts, independence, and
even morality. It has been said long ago that two great things
which parents can give their children as they grow are roots
and wings. Roots take shape the moment a child is born in the
sense of the stability and security they receive through nourishment, comfort, and human contact. These roots deepen as the
child grows through the family traditions that are celebrated,
both religious and social, on a consistent and regular basis.
Here is where grandparents play a very important role. They
anchor the sense of rootedness a child has about his or her
place in the universe. They emphasize again what is particu-
larly important in the family tradition. These roots take on
tremendous strength as the traditions are explained and understood in their wider context of Church and society. But the
roots are to prepare the child as he grows into a young adult to

grow strong wings and properly test them in the flights of independence and freedom.

Parents, teachers, and all youth-concerned people are expected to give wings to all those growing. We have sometimes forgotten this equally important part of growing in a young person's life in our stress on roots. Thus, responsibility should be deemed a tremendous thing early in a child's life. And that responsibility should be substantial at times so he or she will grow in right decision making abilities and self-confidence and good self worth. There is a time when their flight will venture far and erratically. Sometimes it looks like certain tragedy as Jonathan Livingston Seagull adventures are attempted. Yet the rootedness of the person, if healthy and deep, will guide these adventures. We, too, do our part to remind those testing their freedom about their roots. We recall them in stories shared and through our own memories, and any common places and names we share with the young person all of which reminds them of their connections to others and their past. This can be done if we discover some rootedness there in the first place. Otherwise, we must trust a lot to the grace of the Holy Spirit to give that sense of rootedness where it seemingly does not exist.

It is more than a military cliché to say that we all need to get our "wings" at some time in growing up and maturing through life as an adult. We need those wings and need to test those wings even as an adult in order to grow in our own creative energies and initiative abilities. Many adults, after having won their wings so to speak, find a way to give up their freedom. The kind of freedom that I refer to is the freedom to lead others and be responsible for others as well as our own individual actions. Quickly others are blamed, or causes are found to blame, in order to indicate how little freedom was really involved in our behavior. What makes a good youth minister is this self knowledge of responsible freedom. There has to be that spirit of adventure and initiative before good leading can take place.

Often, to the disappointment of youth workers, as well as parents and teachers and pastors, we witness the drifting away from Church of one young person or another. We look quickly to find a place to put the blame. In one sense this is good as it does bring us to a self examination. It brings us to an examination of the structures of programs in which we are involved, to see if these can be improved; to see if they are radically Christian; to see if we are living up to the ideals we propose.

But once this self examination has taken place there is no cause for all the needless worry that goes into this care and concern over young people leaving the Church. That does not mean we ever give up the very strict and bold call to them to come back and to work with us. Rather, we should have a confidence in their own freedom and their own rootedness to allow God's timing in their life for an eventual return to the community's ways of practicing their faith. In fact, the return may be a conversion bringing them to a deeper faith than ever was experienced in the first place.

There is cause for hope. We must be hopeful believers. A study earlier referred to supports this hope. The National Opinion Research Center (NORC) conducted a study of the attitudes of young Catholics in America. The study discovered that there is a drift from the Church among young people in the age bracket of 18 to 30. However, the same study indicated after the age of 30, each year, a certain percentage of the group that drifted away will return. It seems that a majority will return to the community practice of the faith if certain preconditions are fulfilled. First, someone needs to call them back into the community practice of the faith. Second, there has to be a strong rootedness. The good family practice of the faith as well as education in the values of that faith in a young person's life was the most powerful element bringing back the person to their roots and the practice of their faith.

One girl, whom I recall, told her story of drifting from the Church and returning. She said she did not anticipate this at all during high school, nor even in the beginning of college. However, in her new freedom away from home in a distant city and among a new set of friends, a drift began. It was supported by the choices of her friends and it gave her a sense of freedom and power over her own life that she did not have before. At first it was just a simple matter of not going to church, but soon it evolved into disagreements with the teachings of that Church. Five years later a friend brought her to a retreat where she explored her own faith roots and came to a rebirth, a rediscovery, of the treasure she had left behind. She re-entered her faith with a vengeance: studying, asking questions, and volunteering in work projects.

Many developmental people contend that a young person needs this kind of rediscovery or rebirth in their life in all major institutional areas. It might be the family. It might be their country. It might be their faith. In the Church there are many who try to celebrate this recommitment, this "rebirth" through the sacrament of confirmation. However, the debate over confirmation remains in theological circles a divided issue. The early Church celebration of this sacrament had it joined with the sacrament of baptism. Many are pointing out to the Church that we should return to the unity of this sacrament with baptism. There are others who argue that our sacraments honor major decision points in our lives and that it is natural for confirmation to honor the "rebirth," the "rediscovery" of the treasure of faith received in baptism. Thus you see programs moving the age at which confirmation is received from the fifth or sixth grade level up to the junior or senior in high school level. This often becomes a graduation exercise at whatever age a parish may set their celebration of the sacrament. I personally lean towards the older age (either in high school or college) at which such a recommitment can be more maturely made. I offer the suggestion that it might be even better to consider waiting until the person is one year out of school (whether that be high school or college) before he or she is invited to celebrate the sacrament of confirmation in the Church. It may be left to the person to seek out the sacrament after a period of leaving school in order to truly make the conscious inner free choice of faith. The celebration of confirmation can be richer once the balance of "roots" and "wings" is found in the individual's life.

Young people are searching for values that work. But in the midst of searching for values that work, they are also testing the limits of reality and even of the enjoyment that can be had from life. Thus, they look at what can be had from all the worlds in which they participate. A basic question often is, "How much can I have or get from everything I am involved with, experience, or am offered?" Gradually there is a discovery of the emptiness and contradictions involved in all of this and a gospel sense of coming to one's senses takes place. Then concrete choices are made between the offerings of the world. Harmony is sought between the spiritual, emotional and physical sides of living. Life is no longer sought in the horizontal sense of a wide area of surface living, but more in the vertical sense of deep living in the acceptance of limits on one's life. There is real freedom in limiting one's self. Choices create these limits. Once we have set up some limits on our life, and in our searching, and in our freedom, we can be most creative in our new or smaller area of life.

One teacher kept insisting on this fact of living, "When you learn to limit yourself you will be free." I never knew as an adolescent what that meant. But it rang strange enough that I did remember it as one would remember a proverb or jingle from a song; now I know its wisdom is showing itself to me. Marriage is beautifully human and Christian when a person can concentrate loving "daily" with another person. The general or limitless idea of loving can be so abstract and refuses to grow in maturity until it can be concretized in everyday limited living. So it is true of religious commitments where a specific work of love is undertaken. Especially is it true when we freely choose to be responsible and loving in *this* parish, in *this* community of believers with all its foibles and humanness. It all becomes a limiting experience but entirely more engaging of our freedom in that we are faced with real, concrete, and daily decisions which are a joy to make at times, and at other times irksome. But this is part of the essence of being "free for" rather than "free from." The truth of Christian living will set you free if you know and choose your limits.

The searching of the young person or the adult needs arresting at some point in the context of conversion. This may be an inner arrest or it may come from the outside through another person or a particular experience. Conversion is decision about a direction of life. It is more than decision, it is conviction about the way life is, who I am, and where I now want to move. It is both realizing myself and decision to transcend myself. It is a turning to God as the ultimate transcendent direction of my life. Some kind of commitment, authentic and lasting, becomes essential to my life and to my response to God.

We search out and go through this conversion in our own lives and we try to help others towards conversion as well. This is core work for a youth minister. Only the grace of God knows when, where, and how that conversion will happen in my life (its suddenness or its gradualness) or in anyone else's life. But my belief in God's incarnation in the world and in me gives me confidence that I can be an instrument in another's movement toward conversion. And that is why I urge all workers with youth to be supremely confident that they can lead and help others toward a conversion of life. This should be the motivation of youth ministry. For my love of God and His love of me wants to share that and wants a family bound together with heart, mind, and soul set on God.

Theologically, in the last decade the reality of conversion has been given much thought and articulation. One of the best articulators of this reality has been Bernard Lonergan* in his writings on the threefold conversion necessary in any authentic Christian living, and in fact, in any authentic human living. These threefold conversions are a) intellectual, b) moral, and c) religious.

Ideas rule the world. It forms revolutions, changes governments, and even transforms religious organizations. I can only give the most simplistic explanation of these conversions, but hopefully they will serve as introduction to their use in work with youth. I have seen this translated quite effectively into youth talks as well as underlie the process of certain youth work or programs.

The first conversion of a person is usually on the intellectual level. I began with the notion of the power of ideas, but there is more to this conversion than just ideas. It has to do with insight, experiences, and understanding. (Another qualification that has to be made is that often there is going on at the same time of any one conversion the other two conversions. We do not compartmentalize parts of our lives as easily as it is done here on paper. Distinctions are made and priority is given here so that we better understand the workings of conversion in the individual.) Through my life's experience I am captured by the

* *Method in Theology* and *Insight* plus later articles by Lonergan.

notion of something, the insight into something that calls for a change of my life. A change of thinking begins and I start to search reality and to screen reality for ways of building up this new thinking. Openness of mind starts my conversion for I allow others' understandings, new experiences of my own, and new knowledge to invade my life. I try to harmonize this new "stuff" of experience and knowledge with what has gone on before in my life and what I have thought to be real. If it does not harmonize I either reject the new "stuff" (thus no conversion) or I begin to change my way of thinking and increase my exploration of this new way of thinking, reinterpreting reality accordingly (and thus conversion can proceed).

For instance, a person has a supreme sense of his or her own consciousness. There is a sense of awe and wonder about this. That person feels so unique in all of creation and begins to wonder how it all came to be and what it means. The idea that "there must be a God" becomes extremely real for that person. So wonderful is creation and so wonderful is consciousness and so demanding is the cry for meaning that it makes great sense that there must be something or someone "other" that makes sense and gives order and understanding to it all. From this point on, all reality is seen somehow in light of this idea that there truly is a God. Experiences are interpreted accordingly and each new "insight" or "aha" out of those experiences reinforces the original idea "that there must be a God." This idea begins to be buried in the heart, and actions in living take shape to honor this idea.

Youth workers must be aware that conversion cannot be taught. Ideas and facts and knowledge can be taught, or at least shared, but conversion (being captured or captivated by such ideas or knowledge) takes place within the individual both by way of his or her openness to the meaning and implications of such ideas and by way of decision to harmonize their lives according to new knowledge and understandings received.

Often teachers are disappointed by the results of their teaching religion five class days a week and not seeing all the newly imparted knowledge taking effect in the young person's life. Often the frustration becomes worse when the teacher begins to compare his or her students to those who are not attending such a privileged school and sees that there really seems to be no difference in the moral behavior or personal maturity of those compared. True, some studies show that there is not that much difference in the moral behavior or the practice of religion in adult living between those who have had private Catholic Christian high school and college experience and those who have had none. The real difference has more to do with coming from believing and religiously practicing families than anything else.

Thus, pure fact sharing does not guarantee a change of mind even though it is possible. The truth of the gospel still holds out for the ones open to being captivated by an understanding of their faith and being captured by right "ideas" of their faith. That gospel statement is, "the truth will set you free." The reality of conversion should be very freeing. As a word of encouragement to the dedicated teachers of religion classes, it should be noted that their personal witness to their own faith and their personal living of the faith does have a profound influence on the individual open to conversion.

The facts shared and taught are very important, for when the individual is captivated by the "idea" and experience of the faith that is being taught there is deep appreciation in that individual's life for the facts and knowledge thus far learned and a new eagerness for much more. Leadership in that faith then has richer possibility for the individual who has had the advantage of a good education. Confusion is less likely in that person's life, when assaulted by the ideas or convictions of another person's faith which happens to be totally different.

Following conversion of the mind is the conversion of the heart. This is part of the second level of conversion called moral conversion. This conversion speaks to a change in values. From the values which we hold deep in our hearts comes corresponding behavior.

For instance, once captivated by the "idea" that there must be a God, and seeing God's presence reflected in all reality I begin to value that presence. It is good and it is loving and draws me to know and understand more about it. I respond to that presence and to its attraction to know more. My behavior will belie how much I am aware of that presence and how much I am attracted to it. The goodness of my actions will show the goodness I perceive in God's presence and the desire I have to respond to such goodness with like goodness. My loving actions will reflect the same thing. Thus my moral or value conversion is needed along with my intellectual conversion.

One youth worker was telling a quite sophisticated group of high school people that we could know much more than the average person about Jesus, His life, history, Scripture, and Church doctrine, and yet it may not make a bit of difference in our lives. Our lives may not be a bit changed unless we decide two things, first, that I am going to be captivated by all the knowledge I have learned because I want to know Jesus personally, and second, I am going to let my heart get involved because I want to feel and live this personal knowledge of Jesus. He was speaking of both intellectual and moral conversion. Maybe one could capture this call to conversion by the simpler statement, "We need to know Jesus and not just to know all about him." But we need to respond to the knowledge and corresponding values if conversion is to be complete. And that brings us to the third conversion which is called religious.

Religious conversion is full faith knowledge and living.

There comes a point where we stand on the edge of our knowledge and reflected values and we must make a commitment. There is judgment and decision making at this point. We commit ourselves to a future of authentic living of the understanding of God we have and the corresponding values which are part of the understanding we have. The path of our faith has been measured and tested against reality and it makes more and more sense. We trust that in the days and years to come it will make even more sense. There will be greater understanding, and so we commit our lives in that trust. It is a leap into the darkness so to speak, but it is not an unthinking, untested leap. It is absolutely reasonable and desirable. It is in this conversion that life styles are chosen, vocations are established or sought out, and commitments are ritualized.

In our society youth (so too adults) have an inordinate fear of commitment. So many live under the "idea" that you must keep your options open. Things are not certain and so much of everything is relative. It is so much unrealized selfishness, for as soon as we are born we are living by others' commitments toward us. There is the marriage or family that brought us into this world and there is the same family and community that sustains us on through life. Some day others rely on our commitments. It is the nature of responsibility.

The fear of commitment is a tough reality for psychologists and sociologists to track down. It has a lot to do with the affluence to keep our options open. It has a lot to do with a pluralistic society where certainty about a way of living is not easily or automatically inculcated. It has a lot to do with not having role models of happy and sure commitments to follow. Those who are close to us and love us are role models for us. Their commitments are important to our lives both as a source of predictable love but also as ways of living to imitate. We do imitate, for it is the practical way we have to see how we should act and react.

Many experience some form of intellectual and moral conversion but are not able to go any further and make their conversion complete at the religious level. This conversion involves more than just commitment. It involves falling in love with the source of the values we have and the "idea" of God that captivates us—it is falling in love with God deeply and personally.

Falling authentically in love means dying to oneself and entering fully into that "other" reality. Thus if we hold on to a bit of ourselves we cannot fully experience this conversion. That is what makes this last level of commitment so difficult. We wish to keep control of the universe that we have and we fight yielding it to another. However, dying to myself and yielding to the love of God does not mean I give up God's most precious creation in me—my freedom. It means I unite my freedom to God's freedom so that there is a new oneness, a happy and loving union. The movement of my whole being and all of creation is toward union. . . . It is a movement of the created and the creator becoming united. Thus religious conversion is a desirable reality.

Dying to myself means dying to my loneliness and separateness. My freedom is not to keep me apart from God or others as is so often the case (because, we suppose, our freedom has been corrupted through sin) but is to enable me to join myself to an all-understanding, an all-loving God to become more understanding and loving myself.

The youth worker is an instrument in the call to conversion of the Creator to creation even while experiencing and growing in his or her own conversion. Knowing this wonderful call to conversion the youth worker will want to make all those he or she is working with alert to and aware of that call. More than making youth aware of the call of God to conversion the youth worker will want to bring youth to an environment wherein conversion can be facilitated.

All of youth work in my estimation, concerns itself with leading young people to conversion and nurturing the conversion once it takes place. The youth worker beginning his or her work cannot presume conversion in the youth encountered or in those for whom programs are designed. The call to conversion must be present and ever constant. It is to be gentle and loving but yet thoroughly convincing.

For the youth work to proceed well in any parish or institution or city there must be a certain number of the youth at all times caught up in personal conversion to the Lord. It is the grace necessary for effective youth work. It is the calling power among youth, from their own peers, that is necessary. Pope Paul VI was prophetic in this in his encyclical *Evangelii Nuntiandi*. In paragraph 72 he shares how necessary it is to have youth calling youth to conversion in the process of evangelization. Peer to peer ministry is one of the requisites of youth work in any setting. If there is not that peer to peer calling to conversion when the youth worker arrives on the scene, then he or she is going to have to borrow youth from some other location or bring his or her own youth to a place or environment wherein the peer to peer calling to conversion is present.

Some of these environments are readily provided across the country today. Such retreat movements as SEARCH, TEC, etc. are precisely built upon the need we all have for conversion as well as the need for peers to facilitate the beginning of the conversion or the growth of that conversion. Stanford University and Boys Town gave results recently to the United States Catholic Conference on a study of the effectiveness of such weekend retreats. Their primary focus and study was on the weekend of the SEARCH but could be generalized somewhat to other similar kinds of weekends. They found that the weekends really do produce lasting change in young persons' lives . . . that the weekends really do make a difference.

The weekends do more than just save the saved as sometimes is an accusation. Granted, the youth coming to the weekends seem to have a somewhat stronger belief in God and practice of their faith than the overall population of youth. Yet there were deep and authentic changes toward an increase of faith, practice of that faith in worship and act, family life sharing, and new activism in the social justice issues of the community among all those coming to the retreat, regardless of their starting point of belief.

The increased faithfulness and moral behavior seemed to still be on the increase even several years after the retreat experience. However, this increase was almost negligible where there was no follow-up after the retreat. Effective follow-up nurtured the changes and gave direction to the conversion begun and influenced the increased growth in faith and action. The one area that seemed to be least affected was the area of values held in sexuality. Either the weekend does not speak strongly enough to the creation of strong values in this area or the societal values are just more influential at this point of the conversion process.

There is that tremendous need for youth to "get away" to evaluate their lives. Within their own home and school peer groups there is too much power to live and act in certain ways for the youth to seriously consider an alternative way of living. At least that is the case in most young lives. A strong family setting and/or grace always allows for and brings out certain young people strongly Christian regardless of their surroundings. We are so totally inundated with stimuli of TV, music, work, responsibilities, conflicts of a personal nature and other things that any amount of challenge we may receive from an hour's lecture, or a ten minute homily, good as they may be, hardly dents the self preoccupied with all the other distractions. It usually takes a total day away from regular living in order to be open in a new way to what we might hear or experience. That is why a weekend involving nearly three days is important. The first day is difficult for we are clearing our lives of the preoccupations of the week and personal relationships. We can hardly be open the first 24 hours of any retreat. Then the real work of grace can happen if we choose to be open. Reflective listening is more likely to take place and spiritual digestion of what is experienced is possible because time and circumstance allows for such.

Usually the first experience of such a weekend aids an intellectual and moral conversion. I have noticed that, despite the "high" of a youth returning from such a weekend, true change often does not happen until that youth returns to be part of the team of another weekend wherein they must work, and give, and share their own faith to some new people. This is because the second retreat where they are asked to help lead calls them to a kind of religious conversion, a commitment of faith, as well as an act of love for another.

So often I have received calls from parents after the second retreat their son or daughter has participated in, now as one of the leaders, thanking me for involving their teenager in a weekend retreat program. I have received more calls after such a second retreat than I do after the first retreat. There is often the question, "what did they do different this time from the first time, because my son (or my daughter) has been much more deeply affected this time?" The answer—nothing different was done. It is just that now in the second retreat the persons are called upon to commit themselves to help lead others to what they themselves first experienced. They are called upon to do an act of love for others and to take responsibility for others whether in leading small group discussion, giving a talk, or leading prayer, and that makes all the difference. In the process of leading they are forced to express themselves (because they have to do it for others), their faith, their prayer, and various life experiences.

The act of responsibility, of love, and of commitment to others, is a form of religious conversion taking place. Thus the effectiveness of these retreat programs is due to the ratio of old Searchers or Tec-ites (by old I mean all who have just experienced a previous weekend for the first time in their lives) being nearly equal to the number of new retreatants accepted on a weekend. There is work for everyone of the "old" coming back. There are meals to prepare and banners and posters to be made, rooms to redo and talks to prepare. There is the work of prayer to be undertaken for the weekend and letters to be written. The list goes on in order to occupy each and every person who is part of the retreat team according to their talents and gifts.

The primary work of the adult coordinators of such weekends, or the spiritual director(s), is in advance of the weekend, helping organize talks, assigning tasks, and planning the schedule in detail. The adult coordinator theoretically should be able to be completely present mentally and emotionally to the youth present on the weekend now that he or she has enabled a whole group to be responsible for the execution of the weekend.

The weekends do not have to be totally for youth. In fact, the depth of the weekend is more pronounced if some parents (or even grandparents), single adults, religious, teachers, etc. can make it along with youth. The larger world is then represented and youth are able to experience a new oneness and relationship with those they live under in most instances in the world outside the retreat. I have seen wonderful understanding take place and new unity between the generations and toward authority when all ages have been able to share a weekend equally.

After my ordination I was assigned to a parish with a large number of youth who were teenagers. Well over one hundred were attending Catholic schools but nearly three hundred were not. We had no youth coordinator. With a willing and energetic pastor I began to organize a youth program for everyone—whether going to private or public schools. I had high ideals. They were going to learn the content of their faith and they were going to enjoy some Catholic social life. They were going to boost our liturgy in song and other creative ways. I spent many evenings every month visiting homes of the young people, calling them by telephone and advertising in attractive ways upcoming youth events. We had our religious education nights and then we had our social nights with a variety of activities offered such as volleyball, rollerskating, bicycle hikes, dances, etc. The cross influence was good. If they showed for the social events and I happened to mention that I missed them on the religious education evenings they began to see that the two were package deals and would show up more frequently. The folk group got off the ground with real difficulty and attendance on education evenings was better than 50% but never better than 75%. I offered the option of Sunday school courses for those who had to work or had other conflicts on Wednesday evenings. I found that the social evenings actually worked best on Sunday afternoons and nights during the school year and Fridays and Saturdays during the summer.

The pastor was good in getting servers and ministers at Mass from the youth until they graduated from high school. He involved many of the young men around the parish in work projects. For this we had to forego a janitor in order to pay the youth wages. But we had sometimes up to a dozen working part-time around the parish. It was tremendous contact. We had a sister on the school staff who was excellent in getting teenage girls to work in her Sunday nursery and baby sitting service.

All of this might sound like I were bragging or painting a great picture. But the truth was that there was no momentum in any of this youth work within the ranks of the youth themselves. I often headed for the phone after religious education to call, for hours, dozens of youth to express my disappointment at their non-attendance. It was passive-aggressive but it worked to keep our numbers attending reasonably high. Constant solicitation was required as well as the continuous need for new and creative ideas. I knew I would burn out soon at the rate things were going. Too much seemed to be sustained only by our efforts. There had to be a better way.

A sister of one of our diocesan religious communities called to ask what I thought of getting the Search program into the diocese. Years earlier the program had made a brief appearance and then fell by the wayside. I was anxious to see it attempted once again. Thus the first Search was scheduled for a July. How I begged and worked on 30 or 40 high school students to attend. I would corner them individually and work through their parents. I dealt with them practically, promising if they went and did not like the weekend I would not hassle them the following year at all about religious education or anything else. That was relief enough to some to accept my offer. Finally we had a dozen who came along to the retreat.

My gamble paid off. It was a tremendous experience for all of us, and it was important that I attended with them. A rapport was established between us, later to bud into real friendships that last to this day, and for the first time in my priesthood and youth work there was a strong sense of "we are all in this business of Church and God's love together." I no longer had to be a loner in this business of youth ministry. Their influence from that point on recruited others to enjoy their conversion experience, a conversion experience to the joyful fact of their faith more than to a basic belief they already had (though this was deepened, I am sure). The following year's attendance at class went up, social events were planned by the youth themselves and music and liturgy began to flourish. The momentum was caught by some neighboring parishes and thus youth work in the larger community setting became easier.

Regardless of the geniusness of local programs and youth work, it cannot proceed and truly grow unless conversion experiences are happening within the youth group. That then is contagious. There are many avenues of providing an environment wherein conversion is facilitated and to which youth can lead other youth.

The one example I have here was something that worked extremely well for our parish. A former classmate who began along the same lines but accented his program by joining with some neighboring towns, the sisters, and concerned parents, to form an area-wide youth program where youth representatives from a particular city research a topic and plan an evening and travel to the next city to put on their program. That city comes back at another time to do the same for their original visitors. It has produced some mighty fine results and enthusiasm in the religious education programs of those cities. I was a guest lecturer there on a Wednesday evening, and it was one of the few times I had been enthusiastically cheered after finishing such a program. So many other times I have talked to a grumpy audience who are grudgingly present. This group tells me they look forward to Wednesday evening.

The point of this chapter was not to present one specific program or another but to bring to the consciousness of a youth worker the need for "the searching" on the part of youth and their new found adulthood as well as the need to call them to conversion in the midst of this testing and searching. That call must be more than words spoken but rather a community effort to provide an environment wherein a rebirth of faith (or a first birth of faith) can take place. The end result of that conversion is a falling in love with God, and more specifically with the person of Jesus Christ. That friendship needs to be perceived as joyful, as guiding, and most of all, as source of tremendous love calling one to high ideals of living. The idealism of youth welcomes all of this and thus is rich soil for the work of ministry.

Chapter Six

RISKING EVERYTHING

Jesus sat down by the lakeshore. Such great crowds gathered around him that he went and took his seat in a boat while the crowd stood along the shore. He addressed them at length in parables, speaking in this fashion:

"One day a farmer went out sowing. Part of what he sowed landed on a footpath, where birds came and ate it up. Part of it fell on rocky ground, where it had little soil. It sprouted at once since the soil had no depth, but when the sun rose and scorched it, it began to wither for lack of roots. Again, part of the seed fell among thorns, which grew up and choked it. Part of it, finally, landed on good soil and yielded grain a hundred or sixty or thirtyfold. Let everyone heed what he hears!"

"The reign of God may be likened to a man who sowed good seed in his field. While everyone was asleep, his enemy came and sowed weeds through his wheat, and then made off. When the crop began to mature and yield grain, the weeds made their appearance as well. The owner's slaves came to him and said, 'Sir, did you not sow good seed in your field? Where are the weeds coming from?' He answered, 'I see an enemy's hand in this.' His

slaves said to him, 'Do you want us to go out and pull them up?' 'No,' he replied, 'pull up the weeds and you might take the wheat along with them. Let them grow together until harvest; then at harvest time I will order the harvesters, first collect the weeds and bundle them up to burn, then gather the wheat into my barn.'

"The reign of God is like a mustard seed which someone took and sowed in his field. It is the smallest seed of all, yet when full-grown it is the largest of plants."

Gospel of Matthew: Chapter 13

Jesus was most ready to sit down and say "Let me tell you a story, the kingdom of God is like this. . . ." Good stories last, and they reach us at every level of thought and emotion. The kingdom of God is like the planting and sowing of seeds. There are some examples which we hear from the thirteenth chapter of Matthew. Jesus is telling us that the kingdom of God is most gracious in its blessings and somewhat unpredictable. Despite the fact that the farmer wastes much seed on footpaths, rocky ground and among weeds and thorns, the good soil produces enough to multiply his original content of seeds by thirty, or sixty, or one hundredfold. Such is the graciousness of God. Such is the grace of God, which is also like wheat and weeds growing together. It flourishes alongside evil and still is productive; the weeds will be taken care of at harvest time. God's grace can work in us despite the weeds of our life and God's grace can work through us even in a world full of injustice and evil. We need to be patient and trusting to the end. The grace of God is totally unpredictable as we see in the parable of the mustard seed. The smallest thing can become the greatest—a surprise of the kingdom of God.

For this reason we risk everything to minister to others and to the world. We risk not knowing the outcome nor being able to measure the results. We risk the unpredictable. We risk smallness and weakness becoming greatness. We risk wasted time and wasted efforts. And we risk projects and plans that do work and those that turn disastrous, sometimes right alongside of each other. Such is ministry in the kingdom of God.

Having grown up on a farm it is so easy for me to understand the point of Jesus. After several years of drought on our farm and some poor crop yields, in the midst of experiencing another dry springtime, I suggested to my father that he might only plant the lowland part of our farm and not waste another year's seed. He advised me that I had not yet the spirit of a true farmer. For you always sow the seed in the springtime and you do so with abandon, leaving the rest in the Lord's hands. "It is all we can do, we never can predict the harvest." That year the yield was tremendous.

When Jesus spoke of the farmer going forth and sowing the seed and scattering it with abandon everywhere, his audience, close to the land themselves, understood that. You always scatter the seed and then are patient for the outcome, for the harvest. The harvest was unpredictable. Today we have eliminated much of the unpredictability through irrigation, fertilization, hybrid seeds, and herbicides and pesticides. Yet there still remains a strong element of unpredictability. So it is with the surprise of God's graciousness in our life.

God's graciousness always is abundant. We always end up with more than we began despite all the obstacles and wasted energy and materials expended on our part. At His choosing God takes one small part and multiplies it into an abundance that surpasses all the wastedness. And the abundance can at times be overwhelming. The point is this: you can trust God's grace at work in your life, in your work, in your ministry. It will multiply the little and the abundance will show up unpredictably. Trust!

Youth workers and ministers do well being aware of this secret of the kingdom of God. It is a key to loving, enthusiastic, and persevering work. The stories of God's graciousness is not only about the scattering of God's grace within us and our lives but also about how we are to expend ourselves in love and trust. It is trusting and loving with abandon. The seeds represent that which we desire to sow in this world. It represents our talents and our gifts. But it also represents our energies and efforts, all our work and plans. We go forth to the field in the first place out of a desire to respond to God's graciousness first experienced in our lives. We wish to share that graciousness, announce it, and contribute to its continuance. Following upon that desire to respond to graciousness, first experienced ourselves, the actual scattering of the seed represents a great risk. The farmer must give up a part of his sustenance and security when he takes what remains of his grain and sows it for hopes of a definite harvest. He knows that is how life goes on and he has witnessed the previous graciousness of God and God's creation in these matters.

The youth worker can be assured of God's graciousness in the field of his or her dedication. She or he can risk themselves, give up a large part of themselves, to take part in the continual graciousness of God. Thus youth workers are encouraged to scatter themselves upon all kinds of youth, the soil of their efforts. Every young person is worthy to chance the graciousness of God. The unpredictable is there—how God will take some small part somewhere and multiply it thirty, or sixty, or a hundredfold. To scatter means to be generous, sacrificing, and unprejudiced in our love and solicitation of individuals no matter what their background, their looks, personality, or status. It means to go ahead in many different areas knowing that many of these same areas of work and plans and programming may not produce a harvest, but that which will produce will make up in abundance for the investment in all areas.

This business of scattering has a special meaning for those involved in parish or institutional settings where there are various staff personnel with differing responsibilities (responsibilities totally different from those of youth work). The youth worker cannot dream or plan on having others help him with his particular work or ministry if their responsibilities do not allow for such cooperation. However, the workers can be alert to various ways in which other staff peoples' responsibilities touch upon youth and stand ready to magnify their work, support and encourage their work and buy into that work. For instance, a parish visitor may often see youth in hospitals he or she is visiting, or at home settings as that person makes the rounds. Solicit their experiences and listen well. Encourage them to know they can relate well with the youth they occasionally meet. Have them mention your name and availability and readiness to help. This is mutual encouragement. For the youth worker encourages all the parish visitor is doing. This is mutual support in a concrete way. That is why it is so important that all staff related people pray together. First we need to encourage one another in the Lord and then we can more readily do so in a variety of human ways.

Another powerful scattering is closeness with the parish priest(s) if the youth worker is not one already. They do much youth work and ministry even if not intended. First there are all the liturgical celebrations. But every parish priest usually has one area he likes in relation to youth. It might be counseling on an individual basis. It might be appointing and training servers. It might be teaching special classes. It might be athletic events or an evening over pizza or at a movie. It might be a special hobby interest such as electronics, radios, music, stereo, cameras, cars, CBs, cycling, etc. that they would be most interested in sharing with one or many youth if only they were encouraged. Accent this special area of youth interest in the priest and alert youth and parents to that as well.

In their report to the National Conference of Diocesan Vocation Directors at their 1980 Convention in Washington D.C. Andrew Greeley and William McCready pointed out that in the religious attitudes of Catholic youth today and in their religious images the priest is still the primary symbol of the Church in operation on the local level. Youth still see what the Church is and how it is when they see Father. Other ministries are absolutely important we know, but the priest still seems to be primary in imaging the Church in concrete operation. This report was given as part of the study sponsored by the Knights of Columbus on the religious attitudes of Catholic youth in America. The National Opinion Research Center in Chicago conducted the study.

The upshot of this study for our purposes here is that it is good to accent any area of gift a priest has in relation to youth work, it will make the image of the Church so much better in the minds and hearts of youth and really is essential to their perception of all the important community of the Church in their midst. Greeley, in another source, has a few related thoughts on the influence of the priest and a critique of that as well.

"The power of the priest to motivate religious symbolism can be very great, but only if the priests themselves are aware of it. The priest who fails to realize that he is a part of the child's symbol system, misses the first crucial step in being an effective part of the religious socialization of that person. Empathy, likeability, challenge, and the storyteller are all qualities or roles which are part of religious leadership in the local community and they begin in childhood perceptions. Leaders who do not sense that, never get beyond the authority and managerial portions of their jobs, portions which are really quite unimportant to average persons and their religious needs. The same issues which apply in childhood tend to apply in the same way during adolescence. Religious leaders who perceive that they are liked and that they are part of the mysterious story do well with teenagers; those who want to deal only with adults do less well.*

Thus it is to the benefit of youth work to encourage pastors and other priests whenever possible. What was said earlier in this book about building up one another, saying only the things that will support another, pertains to those on staff or in authority as much, if not more, as it does to youth themselves. I believe it was Goethe who once wrote, "If you treat a man as he is, he will remain as he is. If you treat him as if he were . . . what he could and should be, he will become what he could and should be."

As this chapter speaks of various kinds of scatterings, know that there is no particular order. These are not done in priority as is appropriate to the image of the seed scattering of the sower. One reader will find one suggestion to be rich soil for his or her work and ministry and another worker will find the same true of another suggestion. That will further show, hopefully, the unpredictable graciousness of God.

The conversion experiences of weekend retreats or other programs are necessary and have been demonstrated as graced experiences. However, as studies reveal and experts seem to concur, the need for follow-up and local contact is most needed for conversion and religious maturity to have some

---

* *Parish, Priest, and People* by Mary Durking, Andrew Greeley, David Tracy, John Shea, and William McCready, Thomas More Press, 1981, pp. 163-164.

continuity of growth, or even to take firm root in an individual youth life. The youth worker is the important link in this process on the local level. Yet what has been reflected earlier in terms of the need for team work in youth ministry and the require- ment of peer to peer ministry among youth themselves suggests something more. That more which can be most helpful is to have a scattering of youth volunteers themselves among other youth working in team with the youth minister. Many young people, upon some conversion experience themselves and upon graduation from college or after a few years of work, wish to dedicate some time to youth ministry but are at a loss to find the proper avenue to do such work. Their enthusiasm can be applauded but a guiding hand over this enthusiasm is very much required for effective ministry to happen. However, we need a willingness within our Church communities to welcome this enthusiasm and tremendous reserve of talent and energy. Plus the fact is known that religious conversion re- quires involving people in leadership types of responsibility— whether that be personal faith sharing, labor for the kingdom, or a vocation of life.

Many faith denominations have long known the value of a period of volunteer time for the faith among the young adults of their faith. The Mormons, in their ideal of having every person spend one or two years as missionaries before pursuing personal careers, have tapped a powerful resource of their faith as well as cementing a religious conversion in those who take up that ideal. Peace Corps and Vista have raised the social consciousness of many young men and women in our nation and thus they will have a lifetime commitment to social justice issues. Many faiths have a reach-out program of travel for their young people, often during interims or summer vacations, that brings deeper faith commitments to their lives. It builds on the ancient Scriptural truth given to us by St. Paul and made more famous by St. Francis "In giving, you receive."

Some parishes and institutions have made the mistake of hiring or putting on the staff a volunteer youth worker who only brings along enthusiasm to do something. The regular staff people are too busy to aid this person along the concrete path of helping other youth or to train them. They may not have the expertise to do so in the first place. Often the youth volunteer is left without supportive prayer and a sharing community to nurture them along in their own personal conversion. That personal conversion is necessary in order to contribute to the conversion of other young people encountered. Thus it can only be recommended that such volunteers be scattered among the youth of our communities if they can associate with a more qualified youth minister or director, or a conscientious and fairly well qualified adult, staff person, or priest, or have a youth center that can offer prayer, support, counsel, and training on a weekly basis.

The advantage to the youth worker to encourage having a volunteer with himself or herself is that he or she has the beginnings of a ready team, a greater work force, and the immediate peer presence for various projects. Teamwork brings about Gestalt mathematics whereby the whole is greater than the sum of the parts. In other words, teamwork has a more powerful effectiveness than the sum of all the work the individuals of that team could produce working alone.

Another kind of scattering may be to send out youth volunteers in groups of two, two guys, or two gals, to help out a parish staff with youth work for a few months. They could contact homes, visit with families and help organize parish youth events, literally be workhorses for the staff in a parish who needs some temporary help to get some youth programs off the ground. This might be most advantageous to smaller parishes who could not afford a youth minister.

There are some dioceses that do train volunteers for a period of several months and send them into parishes that have no staff person busy with youth programs. This is a tremendous thing, especially where I have seen follow-up work done with the volunteers and where a strong support community is offered to them as a kind of home-base. Usually such volunteers spend at least one year, and preferably two, in such ministry. Often they go on to become full time professional people themselves in the youth work area.

It would be the work of a whole other manual to suggest what should go into the training of such people. A good search of resources now available can yield much in terms of workshops, Serendipity books, Ideas manuals, colleges, youth centers sponsoring training programs, etc. There is a National Conference of Youth Ministry that everyone in youth work should be very familiar with. It is part of the larger Department of Education, U.S. Catholic Conference, 1312 Massachusetts Ave., N.W., Washington, D.C. 20005. In 1976 they published a very concise and useable *Vision of Youth Ministry*. It can be obtained from the address given above. I especially like the stated goals of youth ministry: 1) Youth ministry works to foster the total personal and spiritual growth of each young person, 2) Youth ministry seeks to draw young people to responsible participation in the life, mission and work of the faith community. The vision is as fresh as if it were published yesterday. This same department will aid the youth minister to know available publications and national conferences, workshops, etc. on various aspects of youth work.

In this image of "scattering," the point I have been aiming towards is to encourage the youth worker, or any adult involved in youth work, to use every angle available to minister to youth and call them to conversion. No one theory or way of doing the ministry carries the day in youth work. Every available resource and every available willingness on the part of people must be capitalized upon to build up a particular youth ministry. If something is being done when the youth minister comes upon the scene, he or she should not critize it but use it and transform it. The youth worker often is a "unifier" of things already going on in the community, bringing Christ more centrally into the picture and using the cross influences of different programs already in play.

Having just written about how various things work in youth ministry I would like to suggest a couple of necessary tools of youth ministry that are universal in appeal and effectiveness. They are not new in the least to youth ministry so this suggestion is rather obvious. Youth ministry always does well to employ good and relevant music and good storytelling.

My greatest hesitancy about getting into youth ministry was my own lack of musical ability. I have reflected on this earlier in this book but in a little different context, the context of my own feelings of inadequacy due to a lack of gifts. Here again I felt hesitant about youth ministry because of my intellectual conviction about the need for music and the power of music in effective youth ministry. It was a blessing in disguise for such lack of ability forced me to seek out young musicians, keep my eye out for promising starters, and lead such people to a resource place or person in order to learn effective music to lead youth groups in song. Otherwise I would have gladly done everything myself, and by that decision would have denied greater teamwork a chance as well as denied new people to become leaders with their special gifts.

There are more possibilities for good music ministry than just the good guitar player and singer. Good guitar players and piano players have been and will remain a mainstay of youth music ministry. But what can be done when such talent is not immediately available? Several things. I have seen effective use of sound equipment, stereos and tapeplayers. A sing along with a popular song with some spiritual content has sustained many a retreat and youth group. Sometimes creative slide programs are put to the music in order to help youth enter more fully into the mood and message of the song being played. Sometimes skits or mime can use popular spiritual music as background. This encourages youth to enter the music and sing along in future repetitions of the song. Sometimes a few good songs are used as meditations at a Mass or prayer service several times before sing along is encouraged. One group put together a rag group of musicians using some old drums, symbols, clappers, and a washtub fiddle. They hammered out a beat and put words of a spiritual meaning to such old favorites as *Rock Around the Clock* and *Kansas City*. The audience was encouraged to snap their fingers to keep beat or clap and pretty soon most were singing along even when no particular instrument gave a melody.

Music is such a creative and poetic force that usually after some time in youth ministry one can witness those talented in this area write some very good songs themselves. What a pride a group has when one of their own composes. They readily brag about this to others and thereby bring them to the group. To come to this point is often extremely hard work for the youth worker. But it is such a learning opportunity as well.

Good storytelling is the other telltale necessity of youth ministry. This means more than the ability to tell good jokes. That may not even be necessary. However, some form of occasional anecdotal humorous sharing is important. It encourages youth themselves to share likewise. Jokes, or humorous stories, are one of the most natural kinds of storytelling present to us. Often it is hard to find good jokes or stories that are not put-downs of ethnic people, or a particular kind of person (e.g. salesmen, truck drivers, or farmers, etc.), or that do not contribute to a low image of sexuality, etc. However it is good to model a few good stories that are not part of the usual fare of jokes. Instead of telling a funny story at the beginning of a youth program or retreat, I know this one youth director that likes to engage those present in telling something funny about themselves. For instance, he will have each person, as they introduce their name, tell something like an embarrassing instance that happened to them in their lives. Of course, the team begins such introductions to show that it is good to laugh at oneself.

Yet, the kind of storytelling I am referring to is storytelling that teaches as Jesus did. The stories have a point (as should good music and skits, etc.) or a teaching. Good stories employ good images and analogies in order to paint an imaginative picture out of which a teaching shines forth.

Frequently the story about oneself is employed as a witness for the Lord and through which He teaches. It is usually a witness to what God's grace can do. It is usually fun to tell our own stories. It is one of the easier places to begin in having youth give a talk—encourage them to share a story from their own lives to make a point they want to make or that the program material encourages them to make.

When we turn from our own stories, the next great way of teaching and sharing is to use good analogies and thereby paint images that are easy for the audience to hang onto. Image creation is a form of storytelling, it engages the imagination in much the same way, it leaves behind a sense of a unified whole, and it can be quite easily repeated, and it has a point. Here is where ritual in various religious traditions can become so very alive. They are a rich source of images readily available for teaching. Thus many retreat programs are filled with talks and sharings drawing from the various symbols of the faith tradition. It might be water, bread, the ikon of a picture or statue, fire, candle, posture of prayer, oil, ashes, the image of the hand, or heart, the material from which altars, pulpits, and chairs are made, the book, or one of many other examples.

It might be good to give here an instance of a sharing that held up one particular image and expanded it into a beautiful sharing full of teaching and meaning. It was given by one young team person on a weekend retreat for single people. He used the analogy of a candle.

"There used to be a term more common which we used to describe power in relation to machinery, trucks, and cars, or engines of any sort. It was 'horsepower.' That is one kind of description of an amount of power to get a certain amount of work done. There are other kinds of descriptions of different kinds of power, for instance, candlepower. In the early days of the electric light bulb, it was more common than now to talk of the amount of candlepower a particular source of light generated. It made sense to a people used to the lighting of their homes and streets by way of candles or lamps that had a flame burning on some form of a wick. As we drew further from the reality of the lighting we enjoy coming from lamps and candles and take for granted the lighting of fluorescent bulbs and incandescent bulbs and other variations of these we really do not use the term candlepower anymore. It has lost some of its age-old power due to kinds of heating and cooking systems we enjoy that keeps us separate from the fires of energy that have produced such things as heat and electricity. Yet the return of the fireplace and cookstove have rekindled this natural fascination fire has held for men and women and children alike. Thus I doubt that the image of the flame will ever lose its appeal.

Within our Church candles have always been used through the centuries. Thus candle power is still very much a central image for those of our faith. We light the Easter Candle, we get a baptismal candle, and we hold individual candles at Easter Vigil. The Easter Candle is lit at frequent intervals in the Church year. It is also known as the Paschal Candle . . . reflecting the paschal or passover mystery of Jesus dying and rising for our salvation. Candles are still popular outside of the church building. In college dorms everywhere candles are found and used at times to create the right mood for study or for listening to music or for conversation. A candlelight supper with some special friend stirs romantic and other good feelings. Such candlepower is no longer used much in its old practical ways . . . such as that by which we read, walk, or live at night. We have much better technical ways to create light for those purposes these days. It is used because it has some kind of power for us—the power of creating a mood, or emotion, or spiritual meaning. I would like to reflect a little now about this spiritual power a lit (or even unlit) candle can evoke.

Have you ever really looked at a flame of a candle, at how much it could reveal to you and me? For instance, some people have said that it reflects the Trinity. How? Well, the nature of the fire burning on top of the candle gives off really three realities. What are the three realities? One, you can see a form or shape present even if it is changing constantly. It is very much anchored and has a definite shape and form to it. And it also gives off something called light. You cannot see light but you see by light—which seems like a strange thing but true. It gives off heat. You can see a little bit of the heat sometimes when you see the vapor rising from the flame. But always you can feel the heat if you come close enough to the flame. This explains the reality of the Trinity in a way. The Trinity is one reality just like this flame. But it reveals itself in three unique ways to us. The Trinity reveals itself in ways we cannot see and in ways we sometimes can see. Some people have said that the heat of the flame that can be felt if you get close enough explains the fact that we can feel God's presence if we get close enough, we can feel the Spirit of God present and at work in us. A lot of people who are healed miraculously claim that they experience a tremendous heat in that place where they were healed—often explained as a sign of the presence of the Holy Spirit.

We speak of Jesus the Light of Life, the Revelation of God, the way God reveals Himself in the form we could see. In a matter of speaking we say there is a form to God. We say that God took on form, the form of man, of you and I, in Jesus of Nazareth. Thus the form of the flame can be a sign to us of the form Jesus takes on for us to see in order to believe.

Does Jesus still take on any form? He sure does. He takes on form in you and me and takes it on in all the sacraments. You see, the physical realities of bread and wine is a form. The physical reality of water in Baptism or oil in Confirmation or in anointing, or the ring of a wedding, or the holding of hands, or laying on of hands, or the speaking of promises—are all forms or visible (you can see, touch, hear) realities.

But there is more in this image, this sign. There is the unseen part. That unseen part is the Presence of God at work in us. There is so much such an image of the flame can reveal to us. In the Easter Liturgy, we light the Paschal Candle and say "You are the dawn of life, you are the light of life." We celebrate Christ as the light of life. And there is so much richness that can be found in the Easter celebration when we have honored the vigil of lighting candles. The light of faith has been revealed in Baptism and is part of the ceremony. When the candle is given, the light represents the faith that has now been given this person. He or she can walk by a new path and has been given the light to walk by that new path. He or she has been given the basic tools of grace, a loving family, and a loving community, so that he or she can walk by faith night or day, represented by this gift of Light. That is why a candle at Baptism is lit from the paschal candle, it is a sign of spreading that light of faith.

Taking off a new light never diminishes the original candle's light. Have you ever noticed how you can light from one candle or fire another fire and still another fire and the original fire never got less. And now we have more light. It, the fire, is something that can spread itself completely without getting less. Well, that is like God's love. He can give completely to each one of us and He never becomes less. God does not become less in Himself. Yet His love can more and more light up the world through us.

How easy it is to go on about the image of the candle and its light. Some people say something about the candle flame in relation to the darkness of the shadow at its base to tell us about the mystery of darkness and evil. That is good. Have you ever noticed the shadow that is immediately beneath the flame and candle, at its base. It is a little dark shadow and it bounces around just like the flame bounces around and it can switch from side to side and move in all directions. But that little shadow, someone once reflected, it like the power of evil—it is now chained. It cannot escape the light of Christ come into the world. It may bounce around and move around and fight to move away from its base, but it remains chained. It only becomes unrecognizable and completely diffuse and all-encompassing when the light has gone out. When Christ has gone out of our lives, when darkness prevails completely, it becoces unchained from that candle, unchained from that light of faith.

Then there is the material candle itself. It is usually wax. In order for the candle to fulfill itself it must consume itself. Recall Christ's words, that there can be no new life without dying to oneself.

The wax is not alone. It cannot burn of its own without the presence of a wick through its middle. Some people say this is like the body and soul of each of us. The wax is like our body and the wick and the burning flame like our spirit or soul. The wax gives the candle physical substance and visibility. The flame and wick give the candle purpose, life, and meaning. As the candle consumes itself in giving and sustaining life (the flame, the light of life), so too our body consumes itself sustaining life, the life of our spirit. The flame burns by way of the wick within the candlewax, so too the flame within the body is the soul representing our meaning and purpose in our living.

I'll bet you that I shall never look at a candle and a flame in the same way again. "Receive the light of Christ."

I am sure that this analogy could have been added to by the audience after the speaker had finished. But he was quite creative in using this one image to teach so much. Analogies are just that, analogies. They point out something and they compare things. They are helpful but never complete in explaining such mysterious and deep realities as God and His Church and the mysteries of the sacrament. But many analogies put together unveil increasing understanding of these great mysteries. Thus creative analogies are powerful. They reach a person at whatever level of intelligence he or she possesses, and so can be powerful for every audience, no matter how diverse that audience is. Image is an art every youth worker will want to grow into for effective ministry, teaching, and speaking.

This chapter has invited risk in the part of those concerned about ministry to youth. It has asked for the risk of life, for sacrifice, and for total truth in the graciousness of God. Throughout, the central encouragement of Jesus was taken to scatter your energies, talents, and time over every kind of soil of institutions, persons, and the youth themselves. God's graciousness is not predictable but it is always abundant. Let us trust that abundance, but let us also pray continuously for that abundance. We pray to the Father of us all. We pray through the Son Jesus, and by His Word. And we pray in their Spirit who fills us with the adequacy to pray and work in the first place. We should also pray to a few special older brothers and sisters of the faith who have gone before us and who surely are close to God and would willingly intercede to God for us. First, there is the Mother of God, Mary. She should be our first choice of the saints before us. Her concern for youth would only be supreme, she who helped raise one great young person to adulthood, her son Jesus. Then Joseph we ask to intercede for us because of his closeness to Jesus and because of his part in raising the greatest young person in the history of the world. Then we would do well to pray to the patron saint of youth work, St. John Bosco.

St. John Bosco was born in the diocese of Turin in 1815. He dedicated himself to work among the youth and to teaching. His own young years had been very difficult. He helped to found congregations which instructed youth in both the arts and the Christian life. He was known to have occasionally been a clown on the streets of the city to do his teaching and to draw young people to a place where he could teach them.

St. John Bosco, we pray for your intercession over our efforts. May we follow your example of patience and cleverness. You were a gentle saint. Pray that we be gentle. You were filled with joy and good humor. Pray that our work be joyous as well and that we are always able to see the humorous side of ourselves and our work. You want to give because you first received. Help us, by your prayers, to know the greatness of God we have received so that we may be more anxious to give of ourselves to others. Jesus was your model and source of strength. Pray that reliance on Jesus may grow more and more in our lives. Amen.